T0248121

# NEBRASKA VOLLEYBALL

# NEBRASKA VOLLEYBALL
## The Origin Story

JOHN MABRY

Foreword by JORDAN LARSON

University of Nebraska Press
*Lincoln*

The University of Nebraska Press is part of a land-grant
institution with campuses and programs on the past,
present, and future homelands of the Pawnee, Ponca,
Otoe-Missouria, Omaha, Dakota, Lakota, Kaw, Cheyenne,
and Arapaho Peoples, as well as those of the relocated Ho-
Chunk, Sac and Fox, and Iowa Peoples.

Library of Congress Control Number: 2023013538

Set in Minion Pro by L. Welch.

To all the setters—at every position—over the last fifty-plus years who made Nebraska Volleyball what it is today, one of the greatest stories in all of sports.

# Contents

# Foreword

JORDAN LARSON

Nebraska Volleyball. Good luck trying to explain the magnitude or the lives touched by a volleyball program centered in the middle of America. It's truly something so special and unique, it's hard to fully encapsulate how much it not only means to the state of Nebraska but also to me, just a small-town girl dreaming of playing on the big stage.

I often get asked the question "What makes Nebraska Volleyball so special?" I cannot begin to tell you how hard it is for me to put an answer into words. I feel like you can't fully understand it until you have been to a game.

I remember one of my very first games like it was yesterday. If I can recall clearly, it was back in 1999, when the games were still being played at the Coliseum. I couldn't tell you who Nebraska was playing that night, but I remember it was hard to get a ticket. We actually arrived late and were hoping to purchase a ticket at the gate. We were lucky enough that we were able to scalp tickets. However, the downside was we had to sit in the rafters. It didn't matter to me, I just wanted see what the hype was all about.

The sights and sounds that night were something I have never experienced before. The smell of the popcorn that was carrying through the gym. Of course, you had to get some, just to calm the craving. The pep band playing all the classics, along with the Nebraska fight song. And last, but not least, the fans on their feet waiting in anticipation for the game to start.

One of my favorite parts was watching the tunnel walk as the girls took the floor. That was so awe-inspiring. The way the crowd got into the game, with all the chants and clapping sequences, it was one of the coolest environments I have ever experienced. I remember thinking that night that I knew this was where I was going to play.

That's when I knew I wanted to be a Husker.

Growing up I was always a pretty athletic kid and involved in a lot of sports from a young age. My parents truly valued exposing me to all different kinds of sports to really see what fed my passion. I started out playing soccer but hated getting kicked in the shins, so that didn't last long. I actually begged my mom to let me quit. She wouldn't let me quit midseason because she said I made a commitment to my team and I had to see that through. I always appreciated that about her. Even in my later years, when times got tough, my mom never let me quit.

After not having a great experience playing soccer, I started playing softball, basketball, and volleyball at around the same time, with my parents as coaches. I would probably say at that young of an age I loved them all equally, however at the age of twelve I was presented with the opportunity to play club volleyball. Club volleyball was going to give me the ability to travel and play, but it also meant a lot more commitment. After watching my first Husker game, I was excited for the challenge and the opportunity to reach a goal I had set for myself of playing volleyball in college. My parents were my biggest fans and put so much time and energy into it for me to be able to play. Without them I wouldn't be where I am today.

Almost every summer I attended Nebraska's volleyball camp. My first-ever memory of camp was being coached by

Amber Holmquist. She was so kind and helpful, it made me fall in love with Nebraska even more. When it came time for me to choose where I wanted to go to school, it was a no-brainer for me. For my family to be able to come to all of my games and go to a school the entire state values, that was a true honor. However, with that decision came an enormous amount of pressure and expectation because of the weight of the program's history.

After graduating from high school at Logan View, I was both excited and scared for what was next. I was walking into a program that was currently ranked No. 1 in the country. Not going to lie: at the time I was really doubting my ability. Asking questions like, 'Can I really hang with these girls?' That summer I decided to start summer school and start conditioning with the girls in early June, which I felt gave me some confidence going into my first season as a Husker. I remember getting ready for my first game. I couldn't help but think back on that time when I was just a little girl in the stands, now getting to walk out in the tunnel walk. It was really a surreal experience.

My four years at Nebraska were some of the best years of my life. It taught me how to not settle, to always strive for excellence, how to build a championship team, how to work well with others. It also taught me how to push past frustrations even when things seem out of your control. And, lastly, how special it was to play in front of all the fans. While playing in front of 3,500 (at the time) was intimidating, it taught me how to handle high-pressure situations. I became very comfortable performing at that level and leaning into some uncomfortable moments. Coach Cook always talked about getting comfortable in uncomfortable situations. I think about that often and it still resonates with me today.

While my volleyball career has allowed me to travel all over the world and made it possible to experience many different arenas, nothing compares to playing in front of the Nebraska crowd. They just love volleyball and people making great plays. You don't see that most places.

Nebraska Volleyball set me up for success, and I will forever be indebted to the program because of my experience there. It is truly something so special to me. I wear my red with pride.

# Preface

Jordan Larson had them. So did John Cook and Terry Pettit. And Pat Sullivan before them. And hundreds of others who have made Nebraska Volleyball the big-dream machine it is today. This is for them. For Nancy Grant. For Cathy Noth. For Kelly Hunter, and Kelly's mom, too. For all of them.

This is how it works. You take the Why Can'ts and, like an Allison Weston attack, you ferociously knock them to the floor one by one. First you start with no regard for geography whatsoever.

Why can't Nebraska become one of the top volleyball schools in the nation? Why can't the Huskers win a bunch of national championships amid the corn and bean fields? Why can't a women's volleyball program make a profit? Why can't a girl from Hooper, Nebraska, become the best volleyball player in the world? In the world of Nebraska Volleyball, those big dreams keep coming true.

My big dream was to write about it—to tell the story from Albrecht to Zink, from Stahr to Stivrins. I wanted to properly recognize some of the early ground-breakers and ceiling-crashers—the ones who "toted the water," as Angie Millikin likes to tell me, but not without plenty of love for more recent stars and championship seasons. And I wanted Millikin and others who lived it to tell it.

Pettit and Cook said: Go for it. I could not have done this without their support. No way. Both have been extremely generous with their time and tales. Then I had the high hopes that Larson, the GOAT, would write the foreword. For starters, well, she is Jordan Larson. Husker great. Olympic gold medalist. Nebraskan. But there is more to her story. A lot more.

The pride of Hooper, Nebraska, pop. 832, Larson is a humble native star who has a story that tops them all. By many accounts she represents better than anyone what it's all about. "To me, she is the symbol of Nebraska Volleyball," Cook said.

There is more of her story later on, but how great is it that a girl from tiny Hooper and Logan View High has gone on to be a Husker Hall of Famer and Olympic MVP? I think she aced the introduction. That is sort of her thing, as you know. NU's all-time leader with 186 aces, thanks to a jump serve to beat them all.

To think that as a Husker freshman she wondered if she could really "hang with these girls." That's Jordan Larson. That's Nebraska Volleyball: driven by big dreams and an incredible following to be an elite program each and every fall, seeded with stories near and far, from Plymouth, Nebraska, to Puerto Rico. Stars from Hawaii and Arizona and California and Texas come to Nebraska to play. Five national championships. Sold out every night. Ranked every week. So many incredible matches over the last fifty-plus years. So many unforgettable moments.

The funny thing is, it was actually two relatively meaningless 2019 matches against Northwestern and Iowa that inspired me to write this book. The Huskers welcomed Northwestern on November 6, and it was a "really glad to see you" kind of welcome. NU was coming off a 5-set win over rival Penn State. Another battle against the Nittany Lions. The team also had been dealing with the death of team manager Dane Leclair.

The Huskers were hurting. Honestly, they needed a match against last-place Northwestern.

It was a Wednesday night with an 8:00 p.m. start. My superfan wife, Anna, and I got tickets from a friend, and really thought there might be a few empty seats at the Devaney Center that night. It figured to be a 3-set rout. It was a school night. It was cold. I knew it was a sellout, like 265 consecutive matches before it. But that didn't mean everyone was going to show up.

Standing Room Only. Yep, not a seat to be found. Folks standing in the upper-deck walkways. Packed to the Devaney ceiling. A stranger would have assumed it was the biggest match in program history. Really. It was that kind of atmosphere. Like Stanford was in town. (And, by the way, when Stanford really was in town earlier in the 2019 season, tickets were going for $200-plus on StubHub).

As expected, Nebraska beat Northwestern easily. The match was over in 3 sets and ninety minutes. Junior stars Lauren Stivrins and Lexi Sun led the way. Piece of cake. But how do you explain the fact that everything about the scene—the crowd, the atmosphere, the energy—looked and felt like an NCAA championship match? Because it's Nebraska Volleyball. It's a love story like no other.

A few days later, Anna and I traveled to Iowa City to see the Huskers and the Hawkeyes. The announced crowd was 4,737, about 4,000 more than the average home attendance at Iowa. Yes, there was a lot of red to go with all of the black and gold at Carver-Hawkeye Arena. Yes, the Huskers won easily. But there was more to it. A friendly Iowa fan was sitting in front of us with her husband and daughter. She asked Anna: "Why are you here? Do you have a daughter on the team?"

Nope, just here for Nebraska Volleyball. Simple as that. Easier to get a ticket in Iowa City than in Lincoln, for one thing. And one other: The teenager in the group in front of us was also dressed in red. An Iowa girl who wanted to see the Huskers up close and in person. Maybe the next Mikaela Foecke or Madi Kubik. John Baylor, the longtime radio voice of the program, once shared a similar story from a 2019 trip to Piscataway, New Jersey. There were a bunch of Jersey girls outside the locker rooms, but they were not there to see the Rutgers women. Nope. They were there to get autographs from the Huskers.

That is what this book is about. How much Nebraska Volleyball means to all of us. How there are no meaningless matches. How if football fails in the fall, there is that one Husker team that never disappoints. How there is nothing else like it. How do you explain the fact that Lexi Sun's tweet, announcing her plans to return for another season, had more than three thousand likes in less than two hours? Her Instagram account has more than seventy-five followers. Stivrins is in the same popularity stratosphere. They were among the first to jump on the Name, Image, and Likeness train in 2021, when it became permissible for student-athletes to get paid for endorsements, podcasts, and so forth. They received several offers—perhaps the most notable being Sun's deal with Borsheims, one of the most popular jewelry stores in the Midwest. Both players had huge followings as Huskers, comparable to what quarterback Adrian Martinez or any other stars of the football team were receiving at the time. Same for libero sensation Lexi Rodriguez, who quickly became as popular as any student-athlete on campus—"Lincoln Digs Lexi" T-shirts and all.

Can you imagine the Huskers from the program's formative years, who at times relied on fundraisers and T-shirt sales and door-to-door ticket marketing just to keep the Coliseum lights on, hearing that Husker volleyball players are paid good money to endorse local products and that tickets to see them play go for more than $100 apiece on some nights? Times have changed more than a little, but it couldn't have happened without Kathy Drewes and Peg Tilgner and Vicki Ossenkop and all the big dreamers who got it going.

I am not the most qualified person to write this book, but I felt like someone needed to write it. I have done my best to stay out of the way and let most of the words come from the players and coaches who made it all happen. Thankfully, I had dozens of coauthors. What do I know, anyway? I stumbled into it when I moved from the Kansas City area to became sports editor of the *Lincoln Journal Star* in 1997. Mr. Clueless showed up at the Coliseum one night in November of 1997 and was hooked from that point on.

I was lucky enough to meet a fellow Kansas Jayhawk along the way. Diane Mendenhall has been a great resource as a key star of the story, dating to her playing days in Ogallala, Nebraska, which itself is also a big part of the program's history. Diane was the team's first director of operations and was there with me and a few thousand others in Richmond, Virginia, when the Husker miracle crew of 2000 won it all without one single loss. I was there again in Omaha when the 2006 team became the first Husker bunch to win a National Championship right here in Nebraska. What a big-dream night that was. More to come on the famous Dani Mancuso text that set the stage for that championship (and, as a bonus, became a book title).

My connections other than living in Lincoln and helping to cover the team for a decade or so? I am married to one of the team's biggest fans, for starters. And I know a bunch of Husker volleyball fanatics, many of them volunteers at the Food Bank of Lincoln, where I have worked since 2011. Many of them helped me with this project, sharing stories about their favorite players and memorable matches. Not sure how these qualifications fare, but I spent part of my early childhood in Festus, Missouri (Tisha Delaney country). And Anna and I have had dinner on Main Street in Hooper, so I totally have that one covered. Believe it or not, I went to junior high at Webb School in Knoxville, Tennessee. Y'all know anyone from that area?

Husker setting great Nicklin Hames graduated from Webb, just a few years after I was there. Just a few. Like forty. Hames quickly became a fan favorite and later an NIL star at Nebraska. What a competitor. What a personality. Think Reese Witherspoon with mad volleyball skills.

"I remember watching games with my dad, and Nebraska would be on TV," Hames said, "and I knew Dani Busboom [Kelly]. She worked at Tennessee, and she's basically the one who made me a setter. I heard stories from her a little bit, and I watched them on TV. Dani always talked about just how amazing the state was and how invested they are in volleyball. I don't think I really understood that until I came here for my first visit. When I look back, I was like fourteen when I made the decision, and you never know if you're making the right decision, but this has been everything I ever wanted."

Busboom is a big part of that. From little Adams, Nebraska, to a National Championship as a Husker in 2006 to a head-coaching position at Louisville, where she got going with a great start as the boss. She gets it and is doing her best to create the same kind of atmosphere in Kentucky. No easy task, and she knows it. "The first thing is the tradition [at Nebraska] and what it means to the state and the people in the state. Being some place where it is so important just makes every day that much more rewarding. You have a sense of purpose that's pretty difficult to replicate anywhere else in the country."

My original mission was to tell Busboom's story and many others just like it, to capture fifty years of Nebraska Volleyball in about eighty thousand words. Not really possible. So one book became two. This is volume 1, focusing mostly on the first twenty-five years of the program—before liberos and prematch light shows—and featuring Janice Kruger and Karen Dahlgren (Schonewise) and Angie Millikin (Goodgame) and many other players who built this incredible thing from scratch. Millikin was a star from Ogallala and became known as "Mad Dog" when she would lead the Husker B Team to victory after victory over the first string team in practice, prompting a young assistant named John Cook to say, "Look out, Angie is playing like a mad dog again."

Coming up soon you will read about Kruger and Sullivan, the coach who helped get things going shortly after Title IX became law. As a refresher, Title IX of the Education Amendments Act of 1972 is a federal law that states: "No person in the United States shall, on the basis of sex, be excluded from participation in, be denied the benefits of, or be subjected to discrimination under any education program or activity receiving Federal financial assistance."

1972. Sure seems like a long time ago, and it is, but not longer than the time it took for us to wake up. For men to wake up. It was way past time to end the nonsense, a time when some men still thought women in athletics were just hurting their reproductive capacity by competing. Seriously. It's true. Kari Beckenhauer, a longtime Husker fan who has been an invaluable source of assistance for the book, has shared how much she appreciated the great Dr. Barbara Hibner's efforts to combat the sexist fools of the time. Hibner, for example, was adamant that no one should ever utter the words "Lady Huskers." No. Just Huskers, please. She was also behind the Nebraska Boost-Her Club, which worked hard to give women a level playing field.

I think we can all agree that things are a lot better for women's athletics—at least at Nebraska—thanks to Hibner and Company, but we still have plenty of work to do. Having sellouts of 8,000 for every match is certainly a sign of great progress, but we all need to keep shining a bright light on this incredible program.

A few notes of caution. This book does not contain the life stories of Terry Pettit or John Cook. Both of them have written excellent books about their lives and careers, most recently Cook's *Dream Like a Champion*, written with Brandon Vogel and published by the University of Nebraska Press in 2017. Pettit's *A Fresh Season* and *Talent and the Secret Life of Teams* are also winners. I highly recommend Pettit's podcast "Inside the Coaching Mind" and his poetry ("Trust and the River"). I will be including one of my favorites in volume 2.

If you are looking for a lot of volleyball X's and O's talk, you will not find it here. I am the last person who should attempt any volleyball instruction, so we barely touch on that. You're welcome. And in most cases I use maiden names (with married names in parentheses on first reference) to make it easier to identify the players.

The toughest part about writing this book was knowing when to say when. Apologies to all the Huskers I didn't talk to. I could have done a thousand interviews, I know. I had to cut it off at 130, and I am sorry. I did try to uncover the answers to a few key trivia items: How did the team raise money for uniforms in the early years? Which Husker great intentionally took an attack in the face in practice to help fire up the team? Which NU All-American simply could not do a cartwheel for years until finally accomplishing the feat as a senior? Who are Pettit's and Cook's favorite players of all time?

Actually, we will not answer that one. Those two Hall of Famers are no dummies. They are not going to fall into that trap. But answers to come on those other questions, I promise. I asked fans for your all-time favorite Huskers and you did not disappoint. With dozens of responses that helped me compile the list of beloved superstars found in the next book.

You will hear a little bit of Nebraska football talk, but just a little, mostly as it relates to the volleyball team's success. Elizabeth Merrill, a friend who does great writing for espn .com, shares a funny story about the time, while working for the *Omaha World-Herald*, when she told Cook she was moving from the volleyball beat to cover Husker football. "Oh, so you got a demotion?" Cook asked her, smiling.

There are hundreds of stories. Unfortunately, not all of them fun. Shortly after I started writing this book, kaboom, a pandemic and a postponed season. No volleyball in the fall. If you called up the huskers.com website looking for a schedule, this is what you saw:

> The Big Ten Conference has postponed the 2020–21 fall sports season, including all regular-season contests and Big Ten Championships and Tournaments, due to ongoing health and safety concerns related to the COVID-19 pandemic.

But they played in the spring, and it was very much like playing in the 1970s and early 1980s, with almost no one in the stands. Friends and family only. One former Husker, Dr. Barbara Gutshall, had other things on her mind, like trying to help keep the state's COVID death toll from rising. It was at 2,823 in December of 2021. Gutshall is also Barbie Young, a former high school star in Sidney, Nebraska, now doing hero work in the Nebraska town of O'Neill. Dr. Janet Sellon, the former All-American Janet Kruse, was doing the same as a physician in Lincoln. Both of them doing their best to keep folks safe.

Barbie had to postpone one of our conversations to tend to other important business. Her daughter, a senior at O'Neill High School, was off to Broken Bow for a subdistrict volleyball tournament. That provided a break from the COVID crisis at work, but in a sense the doctor was still on duty, reminding fans that taking off the mask to shout encouragement was not really the safest form of cheerleading. The positive case numbers were rising in Holt County like everywhere else, and Barbie was feeling it. The virus was winning. She estimated she had seen more than twenty severe COVID cases up close in her small, rural community. One friend, a woman in her mid-sixties, didn't make it. "A gal I had taken care of for twenty years," she said.

Gutshall is one of the many heroes of the Nebraska Volleyball story. Now doctors and teachers and coaches and business leaders. All college graduates. Through 2021 every Husker who finished her volleyball career in Lincoln has received a degree. And whether you are partial to Pettit or Cook, or to the classic history of the Coliseum or the dapper new and improved Devaney Center, you can't argue with the success and the love affair. And you can't beat the atmosphere. Period.

"I love the new venue. There is nothing like it," said Lisa Reitsma (Rautenberg), part of the Huskers' first national title team in 1995. "I was in awe the first time I stepped in the building. Anyone that goes to the matches cannot deny how stunning it is. I get chills before the game when they turn down the lights for the light show and announce the players. It is just so cool. But there will never be a place like the Coliseum. It was one of a kind, and the crowd was right there with you. You could feel them pushing you and cheering you on as you played. It was amazing. I loved it. There really is no place like Nebraska!"

Maybe you've heard that before. And the exclamation point is there for a reason. For women's volleyball, there is no place like it. Anywhere.

It has been a blast for me to gather all of the Nebraska Volleyball stories that became this book. There have been many stops and starts during the project, and not just because of the pandemic, though that did lead to a delay here and there.

I sent John Cook an email in December 2020, when there was no NCAA volleyball because of the pandemic, to let him know I was struggling a bit with the book. Struggling to find time to write. Struggling to do justice to all of the dreams and stories that made the program what it is today. Cook's short reply was powerful and to the point: "It is a journey!"

Yes it is, Coach. With an exclamation point. One heck of a journey.

# NEBRASKA VOLLEYBALL

# Introduction

A state treasure. That's what head coach John Cook calls Nebraska Volleyball, and he's right. There are not many major universities that would select the volleyball coach as commencement speaker. That happened, in May 2020, during a pandemic, when those 3,417 Husker graduates all needed a little extra reassurance that everything was going to be okay. That those big dreams were as important as ever.

Cook told them, virtually, the story of Jennifer Saleaumua, a standout outside hitter from 2002 to 2005 who is still one of the program's all-time leaders in kills and digs. Cook didn't want to talk about Saleaumua's stats. He wanted to talk about how Saleaumua, a first-generation college student and sociology major from National City, California, wanted to be the first person in her family to get a college degree. And how she did it.

Cook promised to be there when she graduated. So, despite a stomach bug, he was there on December 16, 2006, when Saleaumua got that diploma. Oh yeah, and that was also the morning of the National Championship match between Nebraska and Stanford at the Qwest Center in Omaha. Cook kept his promise to Saleaumua that morning, and the Huskers won their third national title that night—their first on Nebraska soil.

That was the Dani Mancuso Big Dream championship that Cook talks about often. But when the coach and head treasurer is asked to talk about the most impressive accomplishments related to Nebraska Volleyball, it's not the five national titles that top his list. It's all those packed houses at the Coliseum and the Devaney Center. "The sellout streak," he said. "Obviously. It's a no-brainer. It's unheard of."

That streak of sellouts eclipsed the 300 mark during the 2022 season, a record for NCAA women's sports. Even when the Huskers moved from the Coliseum to the Devaney Center in 2013, with capacity doubling from 4,000 to 8,000, fans kept packing the place, and they still do. Mask-covered faces filled the arena again in the fall of 2021. The move to Devaney also allowed the Huskers to do something else that doesn't happen much in college sports other than football and men's basketball: the team started making a profit, just as Cook promised it would.

"I got hired as head coach in 2000. Back then they had the Beef Club. [Athletic Director] Bill Byrne had me go speak at a couple of Beef Club deals. I was speaking at one of those and was talking about our volleyball program and how we were going to be the first team to go to China, in the summer of 2000, and how historic it was, being a communist country with us going in there. This guy gets up and goes, 'So who's paying for your trip to China?' He said, 'If it wasn't for football, you wouldn't even be going on this trip.' I kept my mouth shut, but I made a vow to myself, walking out of there, that someday we are going to be a revenue-producing sport."

That someday was 2014. In the six seasons after the move to the Devaney Center, through 2019, the volleyball program netted more than $3.3 million dollars and generated millions more in contributions to the Athletic Department. The family of Cecilia Hall, a standout student and middle blocker from Sweden, was so grateful for her time as a Husker they made a $100,000 donation to the university after her senior season in 2015.

It could be viewed as more than a little ironic that in more recent times it's the once-mighty Nebraska football program that has struggled, barely hanging on to a record sellout streak of its own. Cook is a big football fan who hates to see Nebraska's program suffer, but that program's pain adds to his sense of purpose. "I feel a huge responsibility, because if you look at what happened in football, I don't want that to happen to Nebraska Volleyball. We feel more pressure, and expectations, especially because of how much football is struggling."

The volleyball program is living up to expectations and then some, in all facets. "And that's not just recruits," he said. "That's not just the coach. That is a program that has to have great support from all areas, from academics to strength training to nutrition to athletic medicine."

Support, period. The Huskers have led NCAA Division I in attendance every season since the Devaney move. In addition, Nebraska has ranked in the top three nationally in attendance every season since 1990. And now it's a program with more NCAA Division I victories than any other. A whopping 1,433 wins through 2022, with a winning percentage of .841. Only Penn State (.851) and Hawaii (.845) can top that. For many years Hawaii was that one volleyball program with fan support to rival or top Nebraska's. Still, Fiona Nepo (Fonoti) left Honolulu to come to Lincoln.

"We were lucky to get her," Terry Pettit said, "because Hawaii, as I learned later, really put the pressure on to keep her, and not let her go to Nebraska. She stood her ground and said, 'I've already made my decision. Thank you, but good luck.'"

Fiona. One heck of a setter and what a gift for Nebraska—an all-time fan favorite who went on to be part of Christy Johnson (Lynch)'s staff at Iowa State before moving to a coaching position at West Virginia in 2022. That's part of the story as well, as so many former Husker players and assistant coaches have gone on to successful careers as coaches elsewhere.

Russ Rose at Penn State (yeah, he did okay). Craig Skinner at Kentucky. National champs in spring of 2021. Dani Busboom (Kelly) at Louisville, the national runner-up in 2022. And several others, including a few who were part of the program before Terry Pettit's arrival at Nebraska. All contributors to that "consistency of high-level performance" who have built or improved other outstanding programs after leaving Nebraska.

Another statistic that catches your eye: Nebraska has been ranked in every AVCA poll since those rankings began in 1982. No other school can say that. In 2019 the Huskers picked up their one-hundredth No. 1 ranking a few weeks into the season. And they were ranked No. 1 entering the 2022 season. The Huskers are No. 1 at being No. 1.

At Thanksgiving time in Nebraska each year, there is no discussion about whether the Huskers are going to make the NCAA volleyball tournament. It's about whether they will be one of the top four seeds, which would mean a home regional. You get the point. The Huskers have been pretty good for a long, long time, and there is no end to the greatness in sight, not with another star-studded recruiting class entering the program every season. One of those recent phenoms, Lexi Rodriguez, was already making national headlines as a freshman for her play at libero and was honored as the Big Ten's Defensive Player of the Year in her first season.

The Huskers entered the 2021 fall version of the NCAA Tournament as the no. 10 seed and that seemed like a down year, as unfair as that is. The bar is that high now. Michael Voepel, who has covered women's sports for espn.com since 1996, gets it when it comes to the national status of the program. "I think of Nebraska Volleyball as an oasis for women's sports," he said. "It is a big-time sport that gets a lot of local media coverage, that is taken seriously, and makes money. There just aren't many programs like that nationally in most so-called Olympic sports, men's or women's. Heck, even people who know nothing about volleyball are at least aware of the Huskers. They will say, 'Nebraska's really good, right?' Nebraska is also a place that other players want to experience. You talk to kids who play at Pac-12 schools, for instance, and they are grateful for the chance to play in an environment like Nebraska's, because it's so loud and electric. I've heard many opposing players say it was the most fun place they've ever played."

One of those opposing players is South Carolina Hall of Famer Cally Plummer. Remember her? One of the John Baylor All-Opponent All-Stars. What a night she had in 2000, giving the Huskers fits in an NCAA second-round match at the Coliseum. She remembers it well. "The fans are so classy, so enthusiastic, so knowledgeable, so it was an environment where competitors just wanted to be in, and I thrived in it," Plummer said. "I loved it. That's why we do it."

That's why Husker fan favorite Lauren Stivrins, an All-America middle who gained an extra season at Nebraska because of the pandemic, couldn't imagine playing anywhere else. "I've been here five years now, and I feel like I'm like thirteen again every time I walk into the gym," said Stivrins in 2021. "The fact that you get to play in front of eight thousand people every time you step out there, and they're going to cheer for you, win or lose, no matter what you do, they are going to come up to you and say 'Good game.' And they're going to come up to you in the store and say 'Hi.'"

And thousands of Nebraska girls with big dreams are going to look up to you, the way Mandy Monson looked up to her NU heroes. From little Wallace, Nebraska (pop. 347), she wanted to be part of it from an early age. To play in the Coliseum. To be the next great Husker. Monson, who played for NU from 1996 to 1999, gave Ohio State a hard look, but at decision time her roots pulled her back, along with memories of being wide-eyed in junior high and going to Lincoln to watch Eileen Shannon and Val Novak and Virginia Stahr and Janet Kruse. "I think when little girls get to experience that," she said, "just like how a lot of boys want to grow up being football players here, the same holds true for little girls and young women wanting to be volleyball players and play at Nebraska."

Monson, like Saleaumua, was an outside hitter who could play some defense, too. No one had more digs per set (3.27) than Monson before 2000. She gave a lot of "influencers" credit for her success. Like Nikki Stricker. "I loved watching her in college as she was a fierce competitor, but she was also an amazing coach." And Becky Bolli. "Becky was from Burwell, Nebraska, and had a killer top spin jump serve. She could ace anyone, and she was another small-town girl." And Kelly Aspegren. "Kelly was an outside hitter from Callaway. I played in the state semifinals of basketball against her little sister." And Cris Hall. "Oh man, Cris Hall was also awesome. That team had so many great players."

Like so many Huskers from 1996 on, Monson wanted to be the next Allison Weston. "Because it's Allison," Monson said. "She was an amazing player."

Monson and Dani Busboom and Anna Schrad (Zajicek), and a bunch of other NU standouts said it was Allison who was their hero. Weston, a Husker Hall of Famer from Papillion, had Coliseum heroes of her own. "When Nebraska started recruiting me, it was like '89," Weston said, "so that was Virginia Stahr, Val Novak, so a lot of big-name players. It was kind of fun to watch them and then go down to the old Coliseum. Hot. Kind of dark. Lots of history. It was an impressive building. I just remember thinking, 'Wow, this would be absolutely amazing to play here in front of all these people.'"

And then maybe, for kicks, go on to play for the U.S. Olympic team, and maybe be a team captain for them, too. She did all of it. Weston, who ranks second on the all-time kills list at Nebraska, gives much of the credit for her success to another former Husker. "I think the biggest thing was that my high school coach was Gwen Egbert," Weston said. "She was a tremendous coach. She was instrumental in, for one, teaching the fundamentals and just being a huge advocate for challenging yourself and putting yourself in the best position to have success."

Pettit and Cook talk often about the value of having so many great high school coaches in the state over the years. Egbert. Sandi Genrich. Joanne Kappas. Jake Moore. Steve Morgan. Myron Oehlerking. Rochelle Rohlfs. Renee Saunders. And on and on. There were twenty-three NCAA Division I recruits competing in the 2020 Nebraska State Volleyball Tournament. That says something about the quality of high school and club volleyball coaching in the state.

Morgan's career in Ogallala is legendary. Angie Oxley (Behrens) was one of his pupils, and a darn good one. "We all hear about young girls in Nebraska wanting to grow up and be a Husker volleyball player," Oxley said. "Coach Pettit did a great job of establishing the Nebraska Volleyball tradition and getting young girls dreaming about playing for Nebraska. I felt the same way when I was a young girl about wanting to grow up and play on the varsity team for Coach Morgan. He made Ogallala Volleyball a big deal, and as a young girl, I idolized the players that played on varsity for Coach Morgan."

And young girls idolized Oxley and the 2000 Huskers, the one group that never lost a match. What a season and what a story. That team had ten players who were part of Pettit's last team in 1999 and then went on to do remarkable things in Cook's first season as head coach. They overcame hurdles and still never lost. Not once. And they are still close to this day. "I just love those girls like my own sisters," said Amber Holmquist (Limbaugh). "It's a really neat bond that we have."

Holmquist, one of the program's all-time greats at middle blocker, was a Houston prep star torn between Wisconsin and Nebraska. She chose the Huskers because it was a little closer to Texas and because of the closeness, period. "I would say mainly the people are what makes it special," she said. "It's the middle of the country. You have a Midwest type of atmosphere. Whenever we played in California or Florida, obviously they had fans and they love the game of volleyball, but it wasn't the same," she said. "I just felt like it was home, that's what I take from my entire experience, that that's where I was supposed to be."

Oh, the experiences. Holmquist and those 2000 champs went to China before the season and then had another trip for the books when they went to the White House for a celebration visit with President George W. Bush in May of 2001. "The opportunity to visit the White House was very special," said Schrad, who was a freshman that season. "I consider it even more special and unique given its timing, just months before 9/11. I remember we got a wonderful tour of the White House and then had the Rose Garden experience, where most of the media photos were taken. But we then had the opportunity to go to the Oval Office with President Bush. I remember him being very gracious and down to earth. He talked with us about his daughters, who were very much in the media at that point. It was an honor to be there and I think it is even more special since the Oval Office visits don't really happen anymore."

It's a big deal. And you have to be a big deal to get the opportunity. "I think it even caught the Secret Service off guard when he did that," said Lindsay Wischmeier (Peterson), another key Husker who is still part of the program as operations director. "His daughter [Jenna] had just been cited for alcohol possession as a minor. He was very real about it and talked about the importance of making good choices and how we are all human and it didn't make him love his daughter any less. Nothing seemed rushed and it really felt special."

Just like that, Lindsay Wischmeier (Peterson), from the Village of Lewiston, Nebraska (pop. 64), was at the White House. Hard to beat that. Another small-town, big-dreams success story. There are a bunch of them.

How about Brigette Root? Like Wischmeier, a coach's daughter. She grew up in Giltner (pop. 357) and attended Grand Island High. She was a walk-on and a Regents scholar and backup setter who became a favorite of Cook's. She was called into big-match service during a key time late in the 2011 season, after John's daughter, Lauren Cook (West), was suspended following a traffic incident. "When Lauren had that accident, and we pulled her out, Brigette came in and literally won the Big Ten Championship. She beat Michigan and Michigan State here."

"Rooty," they called her. "This was a kid who I thought would never get into a match," Cook said. "She rose up. It was Nebraska Volleyball. She wasn't going to let everybody down. I think that is some of the inspiration that comes from being part of this program in these in-state kids."

There's a lot of pride, too, going back fifty years. Before Cook. Before Pettit. Even before Pat Sullivan, the first coach in the Husker record books. "There are people from that time who are a little bit resentful that people think that Terry was the first volleyball coach there, that volleyball didn't begin until Terry was there," Sullivan said. "And for all intents and purposes, when you look at the entire program, you could make a case for saying that's when it took off, no question about it. But I think the women who played during those small handful of years before Terry got there are very proud of the time they spent there. Sometimes, I think they feel a little hurt by not being included and not being seen as part of the history."

They are very much a part of the history. One of those first "in-state kids" was Janice Kruger, from Randolph, Nebraska. She was one of Sullivan's first players. She went on to do great things after her playing days in Lincoln. Kruger is very much a part of Nebraska Volleyball history, and she is mighty grateful, too. "It was a significant time in women's athletics. Title IX and the battles and the struggles," Kruger said. "It's just a thrill to have been a part of that at the very beginning and when it started to happen."

Kruger and her Husker teammates—the setters for a state treasure and one of the greatest stories in all of sports.

Karch Kiraly, one of the biggest names in the sport and head coach for Larson and the U.S. women's team that won Olympic gold in 2021, summed it up nicely: "If you want to learn about women's college volleyball, your first stop has to be Lincoln, Nebraska." No doubt about it. We just need to make a few other stops along the way. So let's go.

# 1

## Plymouth

To try to properly tell the story of Nebraska Volleyball, and the program's first milestone journey, it seems like a really good place to start with a pilgrim from the mighty village of Plymouth, Nebraska.

Kathleen Ann Drewes was born to Ed and Velma Drewes on October 26, 1950. Kathy grew up in Plymouth, a resilient place in the northeast corner of Jefferson County. The original Plymouth was founded in 1872 by a group of New Englanders who named their new home after Plymouth, Massachusetts. That first Plymouth in Nebraska actually had to close up shop because of conflicts with the railroads over depot locations. As a result, Plymouth was relocated about twenty years later. It was a short trip about three miles up the road to where the village is located today, on the divide between Cub Creek and Dry Creek, on Highway 4 just 15 miles west of Beatrice. It's now home to four hundred residents, roughly the same population as when Kathy was a girl.

Ed Drewes was a self-employed pipe organ and piano tuner and technician. For work he traveled throughout Nebraska and several other nearby states. Velma helped Ed with that work and took care of the kids and the family home as well. The Drewes attended a beautiful church—St. Paul's Lutheran, a landmark that you can't miss when coming into town. Lightning caused a fire that destroyed the church in 1913, but the members regathered and rebuilt just a year later. That's where Kathy went to school from grades 3 through 8. Her first volleyball memories are from those days on the St. Paul's playground during recess. Her brother, Dick, helped her athletic dreams along when he took a teaching job in nearby Clatonia. This was just as Kathy was getting ready for high school. "When he was at Clatonia, he did some basketball and football coaching. They also had volleyball, and they had a year that they were just tremendous, and I was very inspired watching those girls play. That gave me something to shoot for when I got into high school."

Kathy Drewes had the height to match her love for athletics. By the time she finished high school she was a little more than 6-foot-1, so volleyball and basketball were a good fit for her. She loved all of it. On the volleyball court, she was a spiker. "At that time, you had a setter and the rest were hitters. Of course, we called them spikers back then. So you had one setter, and the rest were spikers, so I was a spiker. It wasn't classified like you have all these position titles now."

She was a star for the Plymouth High Pilgrims for two years, in a variety of sports and activities—Kathy loved music, too— but then came change. There were new challenges at every turn for the Pilgrims and the Drewes family. The consolidation of the towns of Plymouth, DeWitt, and Swanton led to the creation of Tri County High, which is where Kathy finished high school. The nifty new school just south of DeWitt came with a big scare. "My junior year, they told us we probably wouldn't see any more volleyball because they thought with all of the schools consolidating the girls sports would probably just be phased out. Of course, all of the girls were not real happy about that so we actually signed petitions to try to get volleyball back in for our senior year."

The petition plan worked. "They let us play our senior year, and then they said girls sports were here to stay because the other consolidating schools around were also keeping the girls sports, so we were overjoyed with that, but we had to fight for it."

That was 1967. That was also when Kathy lost her father to a heart attack the first week of her senior year. Ed Drewes had no life insurance. Everyone had to pitch in to make ends meet. Kathy said her mom worked hard to pay the bills. "She was employed at Formfit Rogers in Beatrice and later at Wasserman Wood Products near our home in Plymouth. The company manufactured pallets. The wood was often heavy, and it was physically very hard work, although I don't recall ever hearing her complain."

But despite the hardships at home, Kathy had her mind set on going to Lincoln to get her degree. She finished up at Tri County as part of the school's first graduating class. She worked at the co-op filling station in Plymouth. She was a waitress at the Plymouth Steak House. Whatever it took, she was going to college at the University of Nebraska. "My mother and brother were so supportive. I also worked as a health tech in my dorm for a couple of years. I graduated with a bachelor of science in education, with a major in vocal music and a minor in English."

She also played some volleyball, but that happened mostly by accident, starting in 1968. "I was enrolled in a field hockey class. In Teachers College we had to take some required physical education classes as well as some electives. I needed to switch to another physical education class due to my music school requirements. I enrolled in a volleyball class. Dr. Janette Sayre, professor of physical education, was our instructor. She talked to me and said, 'You should play on the university team,' to which I replied, 'I never knew we had one.' This was the second year that varsity intercollegiate volleyball was being played."

Kathy signed up and made the team—during what she said was actually the program's second year—along with several players she had competed against during her Plymouth and Tri County High School days. The rest is history. Really.

The coach for Drewes's first two seasons was Ina Anderson, a physical education instructor. Then a young graduate student named Connie Ludwig took over as coach for the 1970–71 season, which turned out to be a very memorable one.

Those Husker pilgrims, with their hometowns, for the books: Jan Cheney (Bennet), Kathy Crewdson (Lincoln), Kathy Drewes (Plymouth), Dee Fentiman (Unadilla), Debbie Knerr (Walton), Elise Mahoney (Mitchell), Pam Rikli Miller (Murdock), Karen Ostrander (Palmyra), Linda Perry (Malcolm), and Peg Tilgner (Daykin).

Last, but certainly not least, in the case of Tilgner. She was the team's setter and a darn good one. Drewes said Tilgner's Daykin teams were always tough. She had a heck of a serve, too. It was almost always on the money and very difficult to return, despite a lack of velocity. "What I remember," Tilgner said, "is that if I served all fifteen in one game, I was under orders to miss after five in the second game or I would be pulled out so other people had a chance to serve. This only happened against a couple of in-state teams that were woefully undermanned. There were people who served harder, but I was more accurate. I could place my serve and it usually had a tail on it like a slider in baseball that fooled a lot of serve receivers."

This was before the existence of digging as we know it today. Before defensive specialists. Before the libero. Every player had to be able to do it all, including help foot the bill. Players had to pitch in and help with travel and meal expenses. They took care of their own laundry and uniforms. Class came first, ahead of volleyball practice. The players took pride in having better grades than the football team.

The football team had trainers. The volleyball team did not. But Drewes and Tilgner both said the head athletic trainer, George Sullivan, and his assistant, Roger Long, would come through in a pinch. Drewes had a bad ankle, from a high school injury, that regularly needed attention. "Roger snuck some tape and taped my ankle," she said. "He'd help me out and give me a little tape on the side."

While the volleyball team did not have the same luxuries as the men's programs at the time—not even close—the players did get to enjoy a brand new facility in Mabel Lee Hall, which was completed in 1968 as the home of women's physical education programs, at 14th and Vine Streets, just east of the history-rich Nebraska Coliseum, home of the Husker men's basketball team since the 1920s.

Mabel Lee felt like a palace, and a van trip to Wayne, Nebraska, for a match felt like the grandest adventure. Tilgner loved all of it. "The friendships and camaraderie were what I remember best," she said. "We had all played volleyball in small schools and loved the opportunity to continue playing in college. That wouldn't have been possible without the help of Dr. Jan Sayre and Dr. Doris O'Donnell, who paid for uniforms out of their own pockets and convinced the department chair to give somebody teaching load credit for coaching. The university did not fund the sport as part of the Athletics Department in those days, which is why the coaches were drawn from the ranks of teachers and professors."

And the players were all from Nebraska. The 1970 crew was led by Miller, Tilgner said. She was a good one, and Drewes confirmed it, recalling how those Murdock girls always gave Tri County fits on the court. "I was told they used to practice with basketballs," she joked.

Whatever they did, it got them ready for the big time for the first time in Nebraska Volleyball history. The 1970–71 Huskers won the Nebraska State Volleyball Tournament, held in December at Midland College in Fremont and then advanced to the national tournament in Lawrence, Kansas. It was a really big deal. "I was calling in the scores," Drewes said. "We didn't have a sports-information person. When we went to Nationals, I remember calling [TV] Channel 10–11, and that was when the Nebraska football team was winning National Championships, and I said, 'Do you know there's another team that's going to Nationals?' I said, 'It's our volley-ball team. Would you like to come out?' And so they did. They came out to Mabel Lee Hall. It was practically brand new."

Everything was brand new, like the pilgrimage to Law-rence. Those Huskers hopped in a van and off they went for a February excursion to Kansas for a three-day tournament that had a name that was also about three days long.

Welcome, Nebraska, to the Division of Girls' and Wom-en's Sports Second National Intercollegiate Volleyball Championship.

"This was our first opportunity to play programs outside of Nebraska," Tilgner said. "We played Long Beach State, Okla-homa State, Ball State, Southwest Missouri State, Texas Wom-en's University, and George Williams College in pool play."

And the Huskers held their own. They went 3-3 in pool play, and the only team that handled them easily was South-west Missouri State (now Missouri State), a Husker nemesis during those early years. Nebraska finished in a tie for eighth overall in a field of twenty-eight. And get this. The univer-sity even foot the bill for motel rooms and meal money—$6 a day per player. A big step from homemade sack lunches and a pool of gas money from the team. The Huskers felt like stars, and they were. The first. Something big was brewing.

Peg Tilgner just wants to make sure people know there was Nebraska Volleyball before Title IX, before official records were kept. And Kathy Drewes wants to make another thing clear: that the Husker team that went to nationals for the first time was not a "club" team. No. Varsity all the way. "We thought we had the world by the tail," Drewes said. "It was just getting the word out that we had a team. And we had a pretty good team, too." Yes, they did, and it started with some roots in Plymouth and a good dose of pilgrim spirit.

# 2

# Off and Running

Much like Kathy Drewes, Janice Kruger found Nebraska Volleyball mostly by accident. Kruger was from Randolph, Nebraska, a town of nearly a thousand people about 150 miles north of Lincoln. As a freshman in 1973 she was exploring the UNL campus when something caught her ear. "I was in Mabel Lee Hall," Kruger said. "I was just kind of checking where my classes would be, and I heard this sound," she said. "I was like, 'Dang, that sounds kind of familiar.' I walked down a hall, and I get in there, and I feel like there's like eighty girls in there playing volleyball. It's the last day of the tryouts."

She asked if she could still try to make the team. "I jumped on my 10-speed bike and rode down 16th Street, got my shoes and kneepads, came back in there, and made the squad. That was the beginning."

Kruger and her teammates were making some noise on campus even though Title IX was still brand new and their volleyball team was still not part of the Athletic Department at the university. The volleyball team was not allowed to use the Coliseum because that's where the men's basketball team was still playing, so all volleyball activities took place at Mabel Lee Hall, named for the university's director of physical education for women from 1924 to 1952.

Mabel Lee, a Clearfield, Iowa, native, was the first woman

to be selected as president of the American Association of Health, Physical Education and Recreation and the American Academy of Physical Education. She made the Iowa Women's Hall of Fame before her death on December 3, 1985. That was the December when Nebraska hosted an NCAA volleyball regional for the first time.

Mabel Lee Hall was not designed to hold spectators like the men's arena, the Coliseum, but it was a perfectly fine venue. In 1973 it was still relatively new. The volleyball team had a perfectly fine coach in P.E. instructor Margaret Penney.

They had talent, too, with the likes of Kruger and Vicki Ossenkop (Highstreet), a standout from Waverly. "[Margaret] was passionate about her profession and loved interacting with her students," said Ossenkop, who spent many years as Nebraska's associate director for recreation programming. "She wasn't highly knowledgeable about volleyball, but we enjoyed working with her and her fun attitude. She was a kind and caring individual who you would have a hard time finding someone who didn't get along with her.

"We practiced and played in Mabel Lee Hall. Men's and women's facilities were not shared at that time, and men's basketball was housed in the Coliseum. The funding for Mabel Lee Hall dictated that they could not charge for any activity held in that facility, so although we had [a few] fans, there was no admission to watch the matches."

It was a start, but they needed more. More funds. More attention. More equity. More everything. And they needed a big-dreams leader to reach the next rung. They needed Pat Sullivan. "Pat was a great educator-coach," Ossenkop said. "She demanded focus and discipline but created trusting relationships with her players. Pat had the experience of coaching in an era that was fighting for women to have the same opportunities as the men."

Sullivan, the volleyball program's first coach of record,

had to fight a lot of tears on the long drive from her New York home to Nebraska, but she says now that she wouldn't trade any of it. Not any of the battles, and there were many. Not even the Run to Omaha fundraiser. Especially not that. "It was an interesting time all the way around," she said. "I was young when I first went to Nebraska. I might has well have been moving to China. My parents lived in upstate New York. I had just finished my master's degree at Smith College. I think I was twenty-six. I get in the car to drive myself to Nebraska. I'm crying until I get to Ohio. I had only been there a couple of times to interview. I had no idea really what I was in for. Everything about it was brand new for me. But I was very excited. I didn't even know who to ask, 'Could we do this or could we do that?' I just did it. There wasn't anybody to say maybe you shouldn't ask your team to run to Omaha to raise money, which would probably be frowned upon, because we didn't do anything that was safe."

Not just the run—a team relay in September of 1975 that raised money for the purchase of uniforms—but Sullivan did a lot of things that were not considered "safe," like fighting for female employees at the university to have a retirement plan. She did that, and she won.

She won a lot, actually. Her Nebraska teams went 114–22 in three seasons, with records of 31-1, 34-8, and 49-13. The Husker record books only show two seasons under Sullivan— 1975–76—but she does want to make sure people know there was a 1974 team, too, and that team, with Kruger and Ossenkop and the rest of them, went 31-1. It says a lot that the "lost" team of 1974 lost only one match that season. It says even more that there is no official record of it.

Because they were so good and wanted to play the best teams in the region, Sullivan's Huskers traveled a lot. They would load up a couple of vans and drive to Minnesota or

Missouri for a tournament and not get done until 10:00 p.m., and with no money for hotels, they would make the long drive home, hoping to make it back to Lincoln before sunrise. "The scariest moment I remember was watching someone drive off the road in a snowstorm on the way home from Minnesota," Sullivan said. "We rarely had the budget to spend the night after a long tournament day and would get home in the middle of the night after winning the tournament. I distinctly remember arriving back in Lincoln as the sun came up. Not sure why no one ever got hurt. Lots of luck going on there." It was all part of the fight for Sullivan.

She got things moving upward with the help of administrators Dr. Aleen Swofford and Dr. June (Jay) Davis and a bunch of Huskers who were excited to be a part of it. Sullivan led the 1975 Huskers to the Association for Intercollegiate Athletics for Women (AIAW) national tournament in Princeton, New Jersey, and her 1976 crew won the program's first Big Eight title.

She said it all happened because a friend told her, "You have to go to Nebraska because it's so different from anything you've ever done." Like going to China. A Nebraska newbie who played her college volleyball at SUNY-Cortland set a nice table for Terry Pettit, and this is the heart of the story, from Sullivan herself:

Madge Phillips, who was the chair of women's physical education at that time, was the person who hired me, so it wasn't an athletic hire. There was no such thing as a purely athletic hire. It was just a really interesting time. Because I was a woman coming into the university in 1973, I went in as a swimming coach, not as a volleyball coach. I actually coached swimming and volleyball for two years. Obviously, no one does that anymore. I'd go off to Big Eight championships in swimming and come back to host a tournament in volleyball the following weekend. It was a little bit of a crazy time.

The fact that we had to raise money to get new uniforms was really a reflection of the times. A couple of years later, things would have changed—certainly at Nebraska. But we were moving through a transition time—and trying to do it quickly—before we actually had money to support what we were trying to do. The athletic director went to the Lincoln business community to get financial support for the team to go to the national AIAW tournament at Princeton University. We were on the cusp of moving from being directed and supported by the women's physical education department to the women's athletic department. Until 1977–78 my salary came from a combination of athletics and physical education. In my last year of coaching at Nebraska I made $12,000. That was not big money, even in 1976.

In those early times, I'm listed as having coached in '75 and '76, and I started coaching there in '74. That point was prior to the hiring of Aleen Swofford and Jay Davis. Aleen was our first "real" athletic director. Prior to that, anything to do with women's athletics was housed in Women's Physical Education.

I don't know if there are records in the state. I don't even remember how many colleges there were in the state at that time in 1974. Obviously, we won the state championship. We played largely in-state, maybe Iowa, maybe some Kansas schools, but we did play thirty-two times. Interestingly, as I moved along, I always looked at my own personal record, because you had to list those kinds of things, as something that is different than what is listed in the volleyball media guide at Nebraska right now. The record for that team in 1974 was 31-1. We had a full record, but we had no sports information director. We had nobody to keep track of anything. But if you asked the people who played during that time, they'll very much say there was a season before 1975.

All of that is just because of changes that were occurring because of women's athletics at all during that time. When Title IX was passed in '72, it's not like women's athletics all over the country just all of a sudden turned into gold. It took decades for things to change. We were, I think, on a very early good trajectory, but for as good as the programs have been all these years, I wouldn't say we were compliant with Title IX until long after '72, maybe in the late eighties, early nineties, I'm not really sure. All that came about because Athletics hired a full-time women's athletic director and sports information director in Aleen Swofford and Jay Davis. All of that stuff started in '75. I count myself as having coached there for three years, and in the last year I was at Nebraska I took an assistant athletic director position and just coached a premier junior club program that covered Nebraska, Iowa, and Missouri, and I coached in that program during that last year, and that was Terry's first year.

Because I was a woman, when I went there I couldn't participate in the retirement system. Only men were allowed to participate in the retirement system. Having parents who very much encouraged me to push that envelope, I pushed that envelope. And as of 1975 or '76, or somewhere in there, women who were on staff or on the faculty were allowed to participate in the retirement system. It's mind-boggling now.

At that point in time the only racquetball courts on campus were in the South Stadium, and I'll never forget this, but there was a big sign that said it was for varsity athletes only. This was like 1975. I thought we were part of varsity athletics, so we would go in, and I'd bring players with me so I could teach them how to play the game, and we'd work on footwork stuff and just have fun, and boy did I get in trouble. It was terrible. "You're not allowed in here. This is only for varsity athletes." This was obviously a time when there was a lot of transition going on, and I said, "We *are* varsity athletes. We are part of the program here." It took a long time for things to change.

But they did change, and Sullivan was a big part of that change. So was Susie Heiser, a standout from Columbus who became one of the first scholarship players—and van drivers—in the volleyball program. "Heck, we were nineteen- and twenty-year-olds who were driving vans in the middle of the night to games," Heiser said, "and we'd rotate drivers every hour."

And then there was that Sunday in September of 1975 when they rotated runners on Highway 6 from Lincoln to Omaha because the team needed money for uniforms and warm-ups. Family and friends made pledges to support the 55-mile effort. Heiser said each player would run a mile, get back in the van, and wait her turn to run another mile. "I don't think any of us on that team will ever forget the run from Lincoln to Omaha," Heiser said. "That was probably the most extreme thing I'd done in my life at the time, but it was one of those bonding things. Yeah, we did it to raise money, but we had so much fun doing it. We would slow the van down, and one runner would jump in and another would jump out. I don't even know how long it took us. It was hours. But I just remember, on Highway 6, running mile after mile after mile. It's that bonding, the way you bond over the sport or the practices, the things that you do, that make you a team. It was just a ton of fun."

Heiser was a star defensive specialist and left-side hitter for the volleyball team and the starting left fielder for the softball team. She was a four-year starter for both teams and, like Ossenkop and Kruger, one of the first scholarship players in Sullivan's program, meaning tuition and fees were covered. Not the full ride that the football players received, with room and board and all of it. Susie's brother Tom was on the football team. That group did not have to organize a run to raise money for uniforms. "It was so interesting the way Tommy was recruited out of high school for football by [head coach] Bob Devaney, and, obviously, there wasn't any recruiting going on for women's anything."

There was plenty of talent, though, with volleyball being the number one sport for girls in Nebraska. Sullivan said that is why it became the leading sport in the movement to make women's sports a bigger deal at the university. "Volleyball was part of that major transition," Sullivan said, "and thank goodness Ally Swofford was a real proponent of volleyball. She was from California. She had good knowledge of the game. She was really supportive."

Devaney had moved from head football coach to athletic director, making way for Tom Osborne to be his successor as head coach. By many accounts, Devaney and Osborne were behind Sullivan and the rise of the women's volleyball program at that time. "Bob Devaney was supportive of women's athletics," Ossenkop said. "There were times of limited financial means, and he stood strong in not eliminating any of the women's sports just because they didn't bring in the same level of ticket sales as perhaps a men's sport."

Devaney hired Swofford and Davis and increased the budget for women's sports to more than $50,000 during Sullivan's time at Nebraska. It was a start. "We don't want to put the males on the defense with Title IX," Sullivan said at a 1974 YWCA event in Lincoln. "Women just want to be on the offense for a change."

Even when things were going well, there were hurdles. The

team still had to go to local banks to ask for donations to make the trip to New Jersey for the national tournament in 1975. They advanced by finishing second at a regional tournament in Columbia, Missouri. One of the team's top players was Jan Zink of Sterling, Nebraska, located just 35 or so miles southeast of Lincoln. Zink was an "almost 5-foot-10" outside hitter known as "Radar" because she always seemed to know where the ball was headed. Zink was a Husker from 1972 through 1975. She played several sports and studied education.

"Both of my parents were educators, so that kind of kept me in the education field," said Zink, who would later coach and teach for more than thirty years at Norris High School in Firth, Nebraska, also not far from Lincoln. "Actually, my twin sister [Jeanie] and I were headed to Nebraska Wesleyan [in Lincoln], and they didn't have a program that she needed so we decided to go to Nebraska. Honestly, I don't even know, unless it was through the PE Department, how I knew about the volleyball team. I have no clue. I think it was probably through the PE program."

Jeanie also played volleyball for one year. Jan played volleyball and basketball and softball. She received an athletic scholarship in 1974, for basketball. The arrangement with the basketball coach, George Nicodemus, allowed her to continue her volleyball career with Sullivan, but Zink said Nicodemus "was not a happy man when I was three months late to basketball."

Zink remembers that $2 a day was standard fare for meal money on road trips at that time. She also remembers the volleyball program budget jumping from $15,000 to $60,000 when Sullivan took over. "That was due to Pat's leadership," Zink said. "She was amazing. She was always so positive. She was positive with us as athletes. She would write little notes to us, to tell us positive things."

The only team that beat the Huskers at regionals in 1975

was Southwest Missouri State. They were not your average Bears back then and are still tough as Missouri State today. Under head coach Linda Dollar, the first women's collegiate volleyball coach to reach 700 victories, they were always hard to beat. "Linda Dollar was spectacular," Sullivan said. "She was a nemesis of mine. To this day, and I haven't coached in a long time, if I had to say what's one regret that I have in coaching, one of them is that the University of Nebraska, when I was there, never beat Southwest Missouri State. We beat some other really good programs, but we never beat Southwest Missouri State. You can tell that has stuck with me for all this time."

Bear problems aside, Sullivan won a lot more than she lost, and the trip to Princeton for the tournament was another big milestone. "We flew to Princeton in 1975. It was the very first flight for several people," she said. "This was a point in time when the head coach would typically be making all arrangements for all aspects of the travel—accommodations, tournament related activity . . . everything. In '76 we flew to California and Texas. Otherwise, either I drove or players drove university vehicles."

Four people to a room was the norm on any overnight trip, Sullivan said. "Not great" is how she describes the travel, but winning the conference in 1976, that was pretty great. "In the Big Eight Tournament in 1976 we beat everyone—best of three, that's how it was done—Kansas, Oklahoma State, Iowa State, Missouri, Kansas State, and Oklahoma. And yes, it was pretty crazy winning the Big Eight."

Also crazy? Driving to summer tournaments in the Runza Mobile, an RV paid for by Runza Restaurants. Jan Kruger said another fine coach of the time, John Walton, would do a lot of the coaching and driving for the Huskers' summer excursions. "It was basically a mobile home," Kruger said. "John would drive, and we would go to St. Louis or Kansas City and compete from 8:00 to 8:00 and play all day long. You drive down the road together for eight hours, sleeping in a mobile home, and you do make some bonds there."

Zink's favorite travel story involved a livestock roadblock. "It was always kind of a journey and a little excitement at times," Zink said. "One time, we were going down to Kansas and it was probably getting close to dusk, and we started up this hill, got over the hill, and all of a sudden there were a bunch of cows out. We didn't want any other cars to hit these cows, so we had flashlights, and we are standing there directing people by, until somebody could find the owner of the cows."

They were all on the road to a place where women would start getting their due, and Heiser agreed with Zink that Sullivan was the driving force. "I have to say that Pat Sullivan was probably the biggest influence for women's sports at Nebraska," Heiser said. "And when Dr. Davis and Dr. Swofford came, because they were from the West Coast, it gave a whole new feeling to women's athletics, that it wasn't just an extension of the physical education program, that it really felt like it was stepping into something different."

Sullivan decided to try something different after three seasons as coach. She wanted to get into administration and took an assistant athletic director role to help get the academic advisor program going at Nebraska. After Terry Pettit was hired as her successor as head coach, Sullivan realized she wanted to get back to coaching and also wanted to get closer to home.

She jokes that she left Pettit with some "good height" on the roster. Pettit will tell you to this day Sullivan left the Huskers' young program in good shape when she left for George Washington University in Washington DC, to become the Colonials' volleyball coach. Sullivan was George Washington's coach from 1978 through 1986 and finished with a record of 289-140.

After coaching she completed her doctoral work and joined the Exercise Science Department at George Washington. She retired in 2007 and now lives in southern Vermont. "My field was sport psychology," she said. "In retirement, I developed a coaching education program at the Massachusetts College of Liberal Arts, just down the road from where I live. All fun."

She left out one key detail. In 1995 she was inducted into the George Washington University Sports Hall of Fame. She made a difference there, just as she made a difference at Nebraska in building a foundation for what has become one of the top programs in the country—men's or women's. "We had a lot of fun during my three years [coaching] at Nebraska, and for their time, the team worked very hard to be the best they could be. Definite intensity. Definite commitment. They were really good."

> I'm still proud of winning that first Big Eight championship. Spending those five years in Lincoln was one of the smartest, the best things I've ever done, even if I've never ordered a Runza online.
>
> Dr. Barb Hibner was the person who took over my position as assistant athletic director and then she went on to have a long tenure at Nebraska and was wonderful. Everything worked out very well.
>
> That's my story and I'm sticking to it.

But there is more to the story. Such as the journey of Sandy Stewart, who was the team manager for Sullivan's Huskers. Stewart was a standout setter for the Beatrice High School volleyball team, which finished in second place in the first Nebraska State Volleyball Tournament in 1972. But a knee injury halted Stewart's playing career. "Pat Sullivan made a huge impact on my life," Stewart said. "I was lucky enough to have Pat as my advisor when I came to Nebraska in the fall of 1973 as a freshman PE major. Having come off knee surgery in the summer, I wasn't able to try out for the volleyball team, but I wanted some way to be on the team. So I asked about being a student manager, and she chose me for that role, which I did for three years [through 1975].

"Sitting on the bench next to her during games I learned so much about the game, but also about how to motivate players. Her positive approach and high expectations drove all of us to be better, a philosophy that I adopted throughout my coaching career—positive but demanding. She was a role model when it came to fighting for women's rights and women's equality in sports, and inspired me to do the same."

Sullivan's boost led to big things for Stewart, who went on to become the University of Iowa's most successful head coach, with a career record of 136-102 from 1982 to 1988. She was the Big Ten Coach of the Year in 1983, when the Hawkeyes went 22-9. "It was coaches like Pat Sullivan," Stewart said, "who paved the way for so many women today to enjoy the benefits of being a college athlete with scholarships, facilities, travel budgets, etc., and coaches that have the staffing and salaries similar to men's programs."

Janice Kruger's story is a prime example of Sullivan's paving work. It was groundbreaking and even life-changing. "Janice was a real leader as a player and had insights into what was happening on the court that other players didn't see," Sullivan said. "She pushed her teammates to become better. She responded to being asked to change positions [as a senior] with nothing but support. She just did what she had to do to make the team better. Nearly forty-five years later I can still see the look on her face when things got really tough on the court. To say that she played hard through every point really undersells her in a big way. She stayed at Nebraska to do her master's degree and it didn't surprise me that she went into coaching."

Kruger went on to teach the game well for many years. After getting her master's in athletic administration at Nebraska, she coached at Platte Technical Community College in Columbus, Nebraska, and then at Nebraska at Omaha, where she went 352-96-6 from 1979 to 1987.

There was an opening at Maryland, and Sullivan and Heiser were among those who encouraged Kruger to go for it. She took the job in College Park and ran with it. Did she ever. Kruger retired in 2007 as the most successful coach in Atlantic Coast Conference history, with 381 victories. She led Maryland to five ACC titles, seven NCAA Tournament berths and was recognized four times as the ACC Coach of the Year and five times as the American Volleyball Coaches Association (AVCA) Region Coach of the Year.

"I followed her career at Nebraska-Omaha with great interest and remember that when the job opened at Maryland I knew she'd be perfect," Sullivan said. "She really had to be encouraged to go after the Maryland job in part because she had so much going for her in Omaha. But she really built an amazing program at Maryland—great recruiting, great hiring, great everything."

Kruger gave the credit to Sullivan. "She just allowed me to learn the game and love the game and be able to teach the game. Pat understood the human dynamic, the value of the person and the caring and also the progression of teaching the game and implementing a plan. She was just one of those coaches I loved to play for. Her influence of being a woman in coaching, and being as good as she was, was such an inspiration."

# 3

## Have Setters, Will Travel

Pat Sullivan's change of course meant there was an opening for a new volleyball coach at Nebraska. The budding program needed someone to keep it growing. Of course, no one really knew it at the time, but what the program needed back in 1977 was a young English teacher from Crown Point, Indiana.

This new chapter in Nebraska sports history started when news of the volleyball vacancy in Lincoln made its way to Louisburg College, a two-year school in North Carolina, by way of a discarded bulletin-board flyer. It was retrieved from the trash by Louisburg women's basketball coach Paul Sanderford, who shared it with the school's volleyball and tennis and golf coach—a young man named Terry Pettit. "He pulled a couple of flyers out of a trash can," Pettit said. "One was to the University of Minnesota and one was to Nebraska. They were looking for head volleyball coaches. I called Minnesota, and they said they definitely were going to hire a female. I called Nebraska and submitted a resume. They asked me to come interview, but they didn't pay for a flight, so it took three days to get there by car."

Lots of time to think things through on a 1,200-mile road trip. Pettit gave it all some major thought. That was his nature. It still is. A thinker and a writer and a teacher. He taught several English courses at Louisburg, from freshman composition to creative writing. He wasn't sure if being a volleyball coach was on the bucket list at the time, but he made the trip anyway, to talk to Doctor Davis and other Nebraska administrators. Players, too. Yes, they put him through his paces at the Coliseum.

"They had me run a mini practice for about forty-five minutes. They had six players that were there for the summer. And I thought that was a pretty good idea. So I did that. Something like that wouldn't happen today, because back then all they were looking for was somebody who could teach volleyball. All the other things that have come into coaching were really way down the list. The only other thing I remember is that the women's basketball coach at the time was George Nicodemus, and he was working with a group on the stage."

Sharing space at the Coliseum was an issue for the women's teams at Nebraska, like most places in the country. Men first, and it was mainly basketball. Wait your turn, Ladies, and all of that. Title IX was still very new. The inequity applied to coaches in women's sports as well. Pat Sullivan's battles were about to become Terry Pettit's battles.

Lincoln hometown star Nancy Grant (Colson) had a front-row spot for all of it. She played for Sullivan as a freshman and was part of the mini practices with the job candidates for Sullivan's replacement. "I remember two," she said. "One was Terry Condon, a UCLA standout who had just graduated, an Olympic-caliber volleyball player. Her tryout didn't go real well. And then Terry came. He kind of fumbled around a little bit. We felt like he knew volleyball, but maybe didn't know how to coach it. I didn't feel like Terry had the greatest knowledge or experience, but I felt like he had a vision. I felt like he was on the side of us as female athletes."

Pettit and that vision emerged victorious. "I went home to Crown Point and thought about it," he said. "They called me there and offered me the job. I thought about it for a couple of days before I really made the decision to take it. At that point in my life, my idea was to take a job coaching volleyball and teaching English at High Point or Guilford. Those were liberal arts colleges in North Carolina. So the idea of just coaching wasn't as appealing to me as that would have been at that time. But I thought I really wanted to get back to the Midwest, although Nebraska really wasn't the Midwest, it was closer. It was seven hours from my home, as opposed to a couple of days from my home."

Was it the opportunity of a lifetime? Maybe not, at the time, but that's what it became for Terry Pettit, who received the following letter from Athletic Director Bob Devaney in mid-June:

Dear Terry:

The University of Nebraska is pleased to appoint you as Head Volleyball Coach for Women's Athletics for one year, starting July 1, 1977. Your salary will be $12,500, and you will be employed on a twelve month basis. You will be expected to coach volleyball and help coordinate this program. This contract may be renewed on the mutual agreement of the University of Nebraska and yourself.

We will be processing a personnel action form in the immediate future so that your appointment will be effective on July 1, 1977.

I am happy that you will be with us and hope that you enjoy your stay at the University of Nebraska.

Sincerely,
Bob Devaney
Athletic Director

Enjoy your stay. Like Pettit was getting ready to spend a weekend at the Holiday Inn. As stays go, this one turned out to be pretty good, and Pettit said Devaney was always supportive.

Not always visible, but always supportive. When it was time to begin that stay in Nebraska, Pettit and his wife, Barb, who was expecting at the time, packed up a couple of setters—one human, one canine—and headed for Nebraska.

"There was my wife, Pricillia, and I, and we had two vehicles," Pettit said. Pricillia was Pricillia Everette, a Louisburg College setter who agreed to help Pettit get things going in Lincoln. "We had a Ryder truck and a Volkswagen Rabbit. Barb and I would drive, and Pricillia would switch back and forth with who she rode with. We also had our dog, an English Setter named Pancho, after Pancho Gonzales, because I coached tennis at Louisburg as well. The Ryder truck broke down in Ohio, and it was a major breakdown, so we had to take a room. We had to wait a day until Ryder got us another truck."

Pettit said Everette, believed to be the first African American in the Husker program, was a fine setter. She was with the Huskers for just one season before deciding to head back home to North Carolina. "She actually started at setter," Pettit said. "We ran a 6–2, and the other setter was a setter-hitter named Sue Luedtke. Pricillia might have felt some pressure there, but she also had a serious boyfriend. She just got homesick." Pettit and Grant both said they didn't think Everette's short stay was the result of being transplanted to a white-dominated community, but Grant did say, "Talk about trying to bridge a cultural gap."

Pettit said there was another issue on the homesick front. A rookie coach issue. "I couldn't give her the attention to deal with that or recognize it because I was a new coach and we had a squad of twenty or so kids. We also had JV. So my attention as a first-year coach there was everywhere."

On the positive side, Pettit said Sullivan had assembled a strong roster, far from an empty cupboard. "The talent I inherited was really pretty good and really pretty deep," Pettit said. In addition to Everette, Grant, and Luedtke, these were Pettit's first Huskers: Lucy Axberg, Connie Bloom, Janet Bornemeier, Reba Govier, Ann Haberman, Kim Hermes, Susie Heiser, Joni Kilham, Marla Lichty, Deb Marshall, Mindy Martens, Lori Melcher, Susan Toft, Nancy Weston, Nancy Wilkinson, and Kathy Wilson.

Ann Haberman (Andrews) was a young player from Beatrice who also played one season under Sullivan. Haberman, who switched from outside hitter to setter while at Nebraska, said playing for Pettit was a challenge, one that she welcomed. "What I recall is that Pat was easier going, for sure," Haberman said. "We were dominating in the Big Eight, but we just weren't competing on the higher level that Terry took us to. I just remember he was a stickler for technique. I guess in general it was kind of fun to play for Pat. It was a little bit more businesslike to play for Coach Pettit. I remember he was teaching a three-step approach to hit the ball. He wanted us all to do the same thing when we approached to hit the ball, and that was new for all of us. We couldn't hit the way *we* wanted to hit. We had to hit the way he was going to teach us."

Grant, like Haberman, was also part of the program from 1976 to 1979, with one season under Sullivan and three with Pettit. She said Janice Kruger was an outstanding mentor as well. Grant was a standout from Lincoln East High. She played for one of the top high school coaches in Nebraska—Myron Oehlerking—and she wasn't sure any college coach would measure up. "Myron was just so gifted," she said.

It took time, but Grant grew to really appreciate Pettit's style as a coach. This is how she recalls those days and her early ups and downs with the new coach:

In recruiting, it was a very stripped-down process in 1975 and 1976. After my junior year in high school and after my senior year in high school I went to a volleyball camp at Lamoni, Iowa. I mean, it was just the greatest thing I've ever been a part of. It was organized by Stu McDole [of Graceland University]. He would bring in coaches from California and Arizona, just incredibly knowledgeable. To Midwestern girls it was just an incredible opportunity. I went to those camps, and I just knew that I really loved volleyball and wanted to continue playing.

Janice Kruger, who was a senior when I was a freshman, has since told me that she was with Pat Sullivan when she came to Southeast High School to watch me play. I vaguely remember that. I don't really remember talking to Pat. I think my father probably talked with her. But I do remember it was my senior year in high school, and two of my good friends and I were at my house for lunch. It was a big deal. We had an open campus at East High. We were at my house for lunch, and I went to check the mail, and there was a letter from the University of Nebraska. I opened it, and my two friends and I celebrated by having lunch. I didn't wait to open the letter until my parents were around. I didn't even call my parents. They were both at work. I didn't call Myron Oehlerking. I opened the letter and I was excited, and my friends were excited for me, and we ate lunch and we went back to class. I had no idea what I was doing. I just knew I wanted to play volleyball. I loved playing volleyball. I had no idea about the time commitment. The maturity level. The self-discipline. I was pretty ill-prepared.

Terry and I had a really rocky relationship my sophomore year. Basically, I had not really had someone tell me what I was doing wasn't enough. He had high expectations, and he didn't back away from those high expectations. A lot of us thought he was unrealistic in his expectations. Honestly, Terry worked hard to figure out how to communicate with us, and each one of us, in our own way. I liked that he had high expectations of me even though he made me angry a lot. And I think at some point I kind of grew up, and I kind of figured out that he was actually in my corner and I could count on him. That changed our dynamics. We went through some painful growing steps together under the big umbrella of Nebraska athletics, of women's athletics. I just grew to respect and trust him, and I still do today.

When we learned that [Pettit] was an English professor and a poet, it was sort of like cool on the one hand, but on the other hand, it was like, oh my gosh, what have we gotten ourselves into? Went to a tournament in downtown Chicago at Chicago Circle. He took us to an authentic Greek restaurant. He took us to Wrigley Field for a game. I was enough of a history nerd that I just thought that was the coolest thing. He just thought about things like that.

In spring ball, we drove our own cars. When we traveled to compete in spring tournaments, we drove our own cars, including Terry. I remember distinctly, that's how I learned how to drive a stick shift. It was with Terry Pettit.

We washed our own uniforms. We bought our own shoes. Our locker room was probably the size of the bathroom in the women's locker room now. We had to take care of each other academically, emotionally, and nearly every other way. What we didn't have provided for us, we had to figure it out, and we did that together.

They also figured out how to win. Pettit's first Husker team opened with a 3-0 victory over Drake on September 10, 1977, at the Coliseum then finished the season 42-12-7, won the Big Eight, and made it to the AIAW Regional Semifinals.

They were learning to fly (and drive a stick). Grant became a teacher herself and had a long and rewarding career, both in teaching with Lincoln Public Schools and coaching, mostly in club volleyball. Haberman became a physical therapist and credits her Husker experience—and team trainer Karen Knortz—for making that possible. And in an interesting twist, and with Pettit's help, Paul Sanderford would come to Nebraska to be the women's basketball coach for the Huskers from 1997 to 2002 and be named the Big 12 Coach of the Year in 1998–99.

As for Pricillia Everette (Burnett), you could make a great book of her life story as it turned out. Sadly, she died in 2018 in Newport News, Virginia. That setter from Louisburg College was "called home unexpectedly," according to the obituary from the C. C. Carter Funeral Home in Newport News, but there was much more to Pricillia's story:

> Pricillia was born on April 28, 1957, in Wayne County, North Carolina, to the late Elijah and Johnnie Mae Everette. She graduated from Princeton High School in Princeton, North Carolina, with honors. While obtaining her Associate of Liberal Arts degree from Louisburg College, not only was Ms. Burnett voted "Who's Who Among College Students," but she achieved Honorable Mention All-American Volleyball.
>
> In addition to receiving her scholarship to the University of Nebraska–Lincoln, in just her first semester there, she received Honorable Mention Big Eight Volleyball award. Ms. Burnett obtained her Bachelor of Science Degree in Physical Education, with a minor in Education from the Methodist College in Fayetteville, North Carolina.
>
> Pricillia was a member of the United States Army Reserves and served for twelve years and received an honorable discharge. Pricillia joined the Newport News Police Department in January 1983. Her dedication and strong desire to make a difference in the areas where she worked prompted her transfer to the Community Services Unit in

1985. While in this Unit, she received numerous letters of recognition and commendations from within the Department and throughout the City. In 1987, she was one of three officers chosen to implement the Drug Abuse Resistance Education (D.A.R.E.) program in the City of Newport News. In her years of service with the Police Department she served in multiple divisions, where she made a difference in the community.

In January 2006, Pricillia was a mayoral candidate for the City of Newport News. In September 2008 Pricillia retired from the Newport News Police Department with 25½ years of service, making her the first African American female to retire in Newport News Police Department with 25 years of service.

In 2010, Pricillia was elected to the Newport News School Board. During her time on the School Board she was the voice for teachers, students, parents and the community to make Newport News Public Schools the Best in the nation.

What a story. What a legacy, and one that includes the fact she was a Husker setter for Terry Pettit. The very first.

# 4

# The Building

Early on at Nebraska, Terry Pettit wondered about the possibility of exploring different trails. "It all kind of happened by happenstance, because I had not really considered being a full-time coach," said Pettit, who graduated from Manchester (Indiana) College in 1968 with a bachelor of science in English. "I thought I'd probably come and coach for a couple of years and then move back into being a literature teacher. I even asked the Athletic Department if it would be okay if I taught a course in English, and understandably they didn't want me to, because they were battling for full-time coaches. A couple of years in, I seriously considered leaving. I went and talked with Union College [in Lincoln] about teaching English there. I just wasn't sure that this [coaching] was my career path. I consider myself a slow learner. I kind of take my time and try to investigate everything about a situation, and it took me a while to really get a feel for it."

But he knew there might be some magic to conjure inside the Nebraska Coliseum. "I became aware that if we built something, that if we created an environment, people would come."

With the NU basketball teams moving to the new Bob Devaney Sports Center, the volleyball program gained more of a single-family home in the Coliseum, which had the history and the charm but still some solar-powered challenges.

The future was bright. At times, blinding. "At that point, the bones of the building were great," Pettit said, "but the curtains were deteriorating and there were some dead spots on the floor. The sun would come in from the west side, and it was difficult passing the ball if you were on the east side."

Pettit had a talented roster. He had an assistant named Russ Rose to coach the jv team. Maybe you have heard of him? And Pettit had the Coliseum, a special place built next door to football's Memorial Stadium for about $350,000 in the 1920s, shortly before the Depression. It was one heck of a gymnasium and a place that hosted commencements and once welcomed swing bands with the likes of Glenn Miller and Tommy Dorsey for dances and concerts. But after fifty years it did need a little TLC. And hot dogs.

Pettit's Huskers started with a bunch of old wooden folding chairs stored in a closet—seating used for things like commencements. Pettit and his wife set up the concessions. They helped set up the nets. They provided key appliances. "Something to cook hot dogs in," he said. "My wife handled the concessions. I remember having a discussion about that, and I wasn't real pleased." Pettit let the Athletic Department administration know about such things. All part of the fight. Sure, they played in the Coliseum, but like Rome, a great program was not going to be built in a day, and it definitely was not going to happen without more talent on the court.

Lori Melcher (Hunter), another standout from Beatrice, was one of the young stars brought in for a boost. Melcher played a key role in Nebraska Volleyball history, first as a player and later as a mom. She credits her high school coach for the assist in battling both her doubts and the elements that day. "She basically said, 'They're having tryouts at Nebraska, and you're going!' I said, 'No I'm not.' She basically threw me in the car."

Her coach at Beatrice High? Vicki Ossenkop. "Lori was

the setter my first two years coaching at Beatrice," Ossenkop said. "We went to state her first year, then we got beat in a barn burner in the district finals by Myron Oehlerking's East High team. Beatrice was the smallest team in Class A at that time. I also coached girls track and field at Beatrice. Lori ran the 50-yard dash, the 400, and threw the discus. She was quite the athlete. I put her in my car her senior year and drove her to Lincoln in a blizzard to try out for Nebraska. Good thing, huh"?

Ossenkop laughs about it but yes, a good thing, for a whole bunch of reasons. Melcher's first year was Pettit's first year. She was part of the group that saw it all take shape. "It was a different situation in terms of scholarships. We technically had to walk on that first year because what Terry did when he came in, he basically said 'This is a tryout.' So we had numbers on our back and those kinds of things. Reba [Govier] and I talk about this. We didn't have any fans. We were just building the program." As well as building interest in other parts of the state. Like Ogallala, which is more than halfway to Wyoming.

"Reba and I and Pettit went out, just to promote volleyball, to Ogallala to run really, really small camps. Even back then the excitement was there." So were the victories. "We worked really hard," Melcher said. "Every time we walked out on the court it was like, 'Well, we're gonna win.' We had kind of a weird confidence."

Melcher remembered seeing Pat Sullivan and the head football coach, Tom Osborne, at quite a few of their matches. Bob Devaney sightings were rare—one match in thirteen years is Pettit's recollection, but Ossenkop recalled Devaney being very supportive, and Pettit said he never doubted the athletic director's desire to make the women's programs a success, even if he didn't show up for matches. "That was fine," Pettit said. "His job was to help find the funding for it."

In 1978, Pettit's second season, the Huskers played a tougher schedule and won another Big Eight championship and their AIAW Regional, thanks to two victories over nemesis Southwest Missouri. Nebraska went 1-4 at nationals and finished 35-25-2. The record wasn't as good, but that was largely a result of facing stiffer competition. "We won the regional," Pettit said, "and at that point Nebraska had never beaten Southwest Missouri State, the dominant program in about an eight-state area. We won the regional and advanced to the AIAW National Championships. Once that happened, the mindset of the players changed a little bit, and certainly my mindset changed."

That weird confidence was turning into something more powerful. The 1979 team won another Big Eight title and finished 41-8-3, falling in the AIAW Regional, which was won by those pesky Bears from Springfield, who also knocked out Nebraska the next season. But the 1980 Huskers got to celebrate the program's first All-American. Terri Kanouse, a middle blocker from St. Paul, Indiana, received AIAW national honors after leading that team to a 35-15 record and another Big Eight championship. Kanouse and outside hitter Shandi Pettine were the first Husker volleyball players to receive full-ride scholarships.

The 1980 Huskers went 18-3 at home, at the Coliseum, where weird confidence was starting to flourish. *I became aware that if we built something, that if we created an environment, people would come.* They most definitely would come. More fans. More talent. All of it. Even without air conditioning. Deb Mueller (Headley), a 1980 letterwinner from Schuyler, Nebraska, remembers some long, hot practices in that building. She also remembers more spectators starting to take notice. "We had decent crowds. Good support," Mueller said.

Also taking notice was a young setter from Parchment,

Michigan, which is not far from Kalamazoo. It was Gwen Pell (Egbert). She played for Mick Haley at Kellogg Community College in Battle Creek and helped that school win two national titles before looking at next-level options. Haley went on to make his mark coaching at Texas, with the U.S. National Team, and at USC. Gwen Egbert—as she is known to most Husker fans—would become one of the most important figures in the Nebraska Volleyball story and, ironically, it happened because the Big Ten, where the Huskers play now, just wasn't very good when she was looking at colleges beyond Kellogg Community. "They were one of the better teams in the Midwest at the time," Egbert said. "The teams in the Big Ten were bad. I was looking at Wyoming. I was looking at Nebraska. I was looking at [Southwest] Missouri State at the time. They were really good."

But she decided she wanted to play for Terry Pettit and Nebraska, in part because it was closer to home than the other two schools. There was only one minor hurdle regarding her official offer letter: by the time she received it, the offer had expired. "They sent somebody like that day to my house to deliver [a new letter] to me, which was pretty cool." So off to Lincoln went Egbert to join Pettit in the battle and in the building. "He had this tiny little office, and it was across the street in Mabel Lee Hall."

And there were bathroom struggles, too. Lots of them. Egbert said you didn't forget to visit the bathroom before practice. "There was no bathroom up on the main level," she said. "We had to go down two levels to go to the bathroom. And [Pettit] did not like you to leave practice because you were gone for two or three minutes because you had to go down two flights and then all the way back up two flights."

Another issue was the showers: they didn't work. That meant players were often marching back to their dorms sweaty and cold after practice. "[Pettit] said, 'You've got to be kidding me.' He was so mad," Egbert said. "He went right over to the football stadium, which is where the administrators were, and just laid into them and said we need showers and we need some towels down there. And the very next day, we had showers that worked and had hot water and towels. We finally had some place to take a shower and didn't have to walk back to our dorm room all sweaty."

Egbert said the university eventually put in a bathroom on the main level, and Pettit was able to move to a Coliseum office. Actually a closet. "His second office was like a storage closet," she said. "They moved everything out of it, and they painted it. There was a desk at each end. It was bigger than the other one and at least it was in the Coliseum."

When asked about the things she learned from Pettit, Egbert talks about setting your sights on the big things and fighting for what you believe in to get there. She often uses the word "fight" when talking about Pettit. "He did a lot of things to fight for himself and to fight for the program."

Like the fight for big-time fan support. It didn't happen without help from the mighty football program. Pettit and an assistant would go to the football stadium on Fridays and post flyers about the volleyball match Saturday. You could get in free by showing your football ticket. "It would take us three hours because there were restrooms everywhere," he said. "We embraced football. I think some schools made a mistake and tried to separate themselves."

Pettit said it helped that he had a good relationship with Tom Osborne. It also helped that the football team was one of the best in the nation. "I think we were influenced by Nebraska Football. On the recruiting trail, if we were out recruiting someone outside the state, the family might not be familiar with Nebraska Volleyball but they were familiar with football. I half-jokingly, but it was accurate, said if you want to build a program that can win a National Championship, and you're a volleyball coach, you either need to be able to look out the window at the ocean or have an I-back that runs for fifteen hundred yards. Either one of those was an entrée into the recruiting process."

Pettit wanted to turn visitors into regulars, so he approached the administration about selling season tickets, to show that the product had value. There was some resistance, but Pettit thrived on that. "I have a saying now that I share with the coaches I mentor: if you aren't getting resistance, you aren't doing your job."

Pettit had a plan and an ally in Dr. Barbara Hibner, who agreed that season passes that would allow several members of the same family or business into a match would help the program grow a real fan base. "I always believed that when I saw other programs trying to build a base, they would have one night when they would try to set some type of record—like Kansas or Purdue—where they would have a match before the first basketball practice, and you might get eight thousand people in. When I watched those things happen, it didn't have any impact for matches beyond that. Kind of like going to a parade. You go to the parade and you go again next year.

"With Doctor Hibner's support, I finally convinced them to sell season tickets. We set ticket prices low. Really, money wasn't the issue. Bring your kids and neighbor kids to the game. I took off a summer and went to HR departments at various businesses."

Pettit usually went out by himself, but occasionally he would bring a player along for the sales calls. He knew that a marketing intern might not have as much success as having the head coach and possibly a player tagging along. "At Bryan Hospital I met with the HR person, to persuade them to buy twenty season tickets and make them available to employees for free. We went to several businesses. I only had one place turn me down. It was a place called The Post and Nickel, a clothing store. Their clientele was the university, college kids. They wouldn't buy one ticket. So I never shopped there again."

Pettit loved the potential of the Coliseum, "one of the better buildings on campus," he said. It even became the focal point of the program's logo, designed with the help of Ross Greathouse of Greathouse Design. Pettit wryly recalls that it just "took some time to get the karate people off the stage while we were playing." But they did that, and the dimensions of the building and the court were nearly perfect for the atmosphere Pettit wanted to create. "We played on that, in sizing the banners, in how the court was lit. The court was lit like a boxing match. Everything we did was with intention."

It was like a boxing match. All of it. The gloves were on. "He had to fight for a lot of things," Egbert said of her coach. "It just didn't happen overnight."

# 5

# Rhymes with Growth

In 1981 Diana Spencer became a royal princess and the shuttle *Columbia* made it into space. The first shuttle mission was a success. Nebraska Volleyball was also reaching new heights with Terry Pettit's sights set on an NCAA Tournament berth.

It didn't happen that year, and Egbert says that experience was painful. "It was devasting for our seniors that we didn't get in," she says. The Huskers were not selected for the field of thirty-two picked for the very first NCAA Women's Volleyball Tournament despite a 29-10 record. "Coach Pettit was so mad that we didn't get in," Egbert said. "He was not happy. We were all not happy. We had all come back early from Thanksgiving break to start training again. The bids came out, and we didn't get one. The inside story was that there was someone on the committee who didn't think we were good enough."

But Pettit and the Huskers knew the only way to move forward was to make it nonnegotiable the next time. They also had a new addition in 1981 who would help with that growth in a program-changing way. Cathy Noth.

When Noth, a multisport superstar from Bettendorf, Iowa, was looking at colleges, it was a time when recruits were allowed to actually participate in a practice with prospective teams. "There was literally a tryout," Pettit said. "She was 5-foot-8 and went up and grabbed the rim. That's all I needed to see."

Creighton was also in the picture, but Noth chose Nebraska. And the rest, as they say, . . .

"Cathy, above everyone else," Pettit said, "was the key player in Nebraska Volleyball development." When Noth became a Husker, the program was able to award twelve scholarships for the first time. She joined Pettit just as things were really starting to take off. She came with rocket boosters. "She came in and was dynamic," Pettit said. "She was MVP of the conference her first two years as an outside hitter. And then I made the decision to train her as a setter-hitter because we were playing a 6–2 offense."

Hitter. Setter. Olympian. Coach. Cathy Noth really did it all at Nebraska. She even played instructor to the team's play-by-play announcer, but tune in later for more on that story. When folks talk about the importance of kids being involved in a variety of sports and activities—not specializing too early—Noth is the poster child for that, during her time at Bettendorf High.

She played middle in volleyball for the Bulldogs and was a forward on the school's 6-on-6 basketball team. She ran the 200, the 400, and the mile relay. She was even part of a sprint medley state championship team. And she was a softball star, too. Shortstop, of course. She hit over .300 in her first season of high school ball (as an eighth-grader). So how did she get to Nebraska? Let's let her share that:

You know, it takes a village, and I was blessed to have good coaches along the way. My mother [Joann] had died when I was ten, and athletics seemed to be where I was most talented. I could pick up any kind of ball and shoot it and throw it and hit it. I had that gift, and I always thought God gave it to me just to keep my dad [George] busy because we had lost Mom.

So then in fourth grade, that's when the high school coaches started to see me and see my athletic ability and how I was a competitor. And through kind of a rec league in Bettendorf, Iowa, playing softball, a high school coach [Gary Roberson] saw me and knew of my talents. So once I got to high school, I played softball for him and I ran track for him. My volleyball coach [Diane Hill] was kind of my mentor. She was a female coach, and she was always so supportive and kind of understood that I was in a house that was not led by a mom. So she became a great role model for me.

In basketball I played 6-on-6 half-court basketball. It was amazing. We would fill the place for the state tournament in Urbandale, Iowa, with like twenty thousand fans. My high school coach was Bruce Rasmussen, who became the AD at Creighton. So I certainly had numerous coaches prepare the way for me just with their coaching philosophy of being positive and pushing yourself and being able to mentally say to yourself you can do it.

And I guess to that point I knew I was gifted and just loved playing sports. It just gave me a great feeling of "Wow, this is so much fun and I am so grateful for it." So I would say fourth grade, that's kind of where it started, and the rumor mill started. Let's watch out for this girl. When I was in fourth grade I wrote down that I wanted to be on an Olympic team of some sort, so in college the only thought I had was what school is going to get me there, what school is going to help me with that stepping stone to that level.

We had a Midwest Juniors club that had Mary Buysse on it, Julie Hermann on it, myself. It was made up of Midwest kids, and that's where Terry saw me, and so did Creighton, who wanted to recruit me for softball so I could play softball and volleyball. And I almost took that, because I loved softball too. But certainly when I went to Nebraska and saw how big it was and Terry, as he was talking to me, kind of knowing my goals. I remember asking him about softball. He goes, "Let's just wait after one year, Cathy. We'll see what your thoughts are about softball." I forgot about it after that. It was all volleyball after that, so that's kind of where it started.

Things started to take off in a big way when Noth joined the program, but she does recall the Coliseum challenges. Those challenges created winning bonds. "We had the small locker room, probably the size of a small living room, and one toilet," she said. "You had to yell 'Flush!' if someone was in the shower. We did our own laundry. We set up our nets. We put out the folding chairs. That's all we knew. And most of my teammates were Midwest girls, all-sport athletes. We were just grinding. This is what we do."

And no one grinded like Noth. "Great teammate," Egbert said. "Worked really hard. In fact, we used to have to run these sprints, with [assistant] John Corbelli. We ran them in sets of ten. We would do six sets of ten, and she [Noth] was always first. Cathy and Julie Hermann. I was told I was supposed to be first. I never got that part."

Erin Dean was also one of the top runners on the team, according to Noth, who jokes about how the running didn't go over so well for one of her teammates. "We had to run a mile and a half in under eleven minutes, and Shandi Pettine couldn't do it. She could run it till the cows came home, but she wasn't able to get under eleven. Shandi's attitude was like 'The heck with it, I'm not gonna get it.'"

And the running didn't go so well for the head coach, either. "We'd always have to run down to the stage and back," Noth said. "Terry decided to run with us, and he pulled his hamstring. I laugh now, but in hindsight, that was his main injury when I was coaching. He snapped his hamstring."

Noth and the other grinders made their big move in 1982, making the NCAA Tournament for the first time in program history. It was the start of a run that had reached appearances in thirty-eight years in 2021. It also alleviated some of the pain from the 1981 disappointment.

Because Pettit and Russ Rose didn't see eye-to-eye on a few things when they worked together at Nebraska, it just had to be that the Huskers would face Rose and Penn State in the first round at the Coliseum. A big-time rivalry was taking shape. And NU played a spectacular match that night. Egbert said everybody was on, fired up to ease the coach's nerves.

"Coach Pettit was very nervous about the match because it was our first chance to be in the NCAA Tournament," Egbert said. "Nebraska really promoted it and marketed it. We had a big crowd. I remember the upper level at the Coliseum was pretty full of people. I was shocked. I wanted to win an NCAA Tournament game because it was the very first time for us. I really wanted to win. We played really well and smoked them in three . . . I remember that, and I remember the crowd really got into it. They were really loud, and Pettit was really happy after we won that. Really happy. I was happy, too."

That put the Huskers in the Sweet 16, where they lost to Purdue 3–2 in West Lafayette, Indiana. "I remember Erin Dean had a really good match [against Purdue]," Egbert said. "She played really well. We all played well against Penn State. Purdue was a lot more challenging." But the season was considered a success, thanks to that win over the Nittany Lions. Egbert said that was a season-maker for the team and for Pettit. "He was over the moon. Oh, he was so happy. I think he hugged each one of us."

Having Noth for two more seasons added to that joy, and

set the course for her to become the first Husker to make Team USA. "Training her as a setter allowed her, at that size, to play for the U.S. national team," Pettit said. "That indicated some growth on my part, in that I had made the decision I wanted an extraordinary athlete at the setter position. From then on, that's all we went after. There were several setters we trained who really had very limited setter backgrounds. You would have difficulty doing that today, but I think we understood the importance of having an athlete at that position. An exceptional athlete." An exceptional athlete with an exceptional legacy at Nebraska. Noth was the Husker's first AVCA All-American—a first-teamer as a junior and second as a senior. A great hitter and setter, she finished her playing career with a nifty .398 as a senior, the highest attack percentage in Nebraska and Big Eight history at the time. She was the first player with 1,000 kills in program history.

Her last match as a Husker player came in the NCAA Mideast Regional final at Western Michigan. It was against University of the Pacific, and the crowd was really into it, hoping to see the Midwesterners pull off the upset. "We were in Kalamazoo and we couldn't even hear ourselves because the crowd was going crazy," Noth said. "Julie Hermann and I were in the bathroom, and we were so nervous because the crowd was just on top of us. I go, 'Julie, let's pray.' So we prayed before we went out to play, and we lost in four."

Maybe the prayers weren't quite enough that day, but for the growth of a player and a program, it was a monumental time. Four years later, in 1988, Noth became the first Husker to make the U.S. Olympic Team, as an alternate. She said it was all Pettit's doing. "I was not a setter. He trained me up after my sophomore year. I was on the fast track. But he saw something in me. That certainly helped my confidence and believing that 'Yes, I can do this.' I'm not sure where I would have been had I not been transitioned into a setter. I believe with my height and so forth, I would not have had that possibility to be on the Olympic team. So yeah, there's a plan, and it worked out great."

She is also grateful for the tough times for women's sports. Yes, grateful. "If you let the disadvantages get to you, then your purpose is not as meaningful. We said 'We are good athletes, and we are in it to win.' And, yes, we had barriers. We had to set up our own chairs. We had to run guys off the court because they were playing basketball. But we were confident doing it. We were like 'Get off the court. This is our court.'"

Thanks to Noth and the players of that time, the Huskers eventually owned the Coliseum. "When I see Nebraska Volleyball, what comes to mind is how hard they work, how hard they work together. How their communication on the court, again, going back to, 'We have a mission.' And that was created, certainly, back when I was playing and got stronger and stronger throughout the years."

Noth also played a key creative role in the making of the famous George Lundeen Nebraska Volleyball statue that is now at the Devaney Center. Lundeen's statue features three players and was dedicated in 1992. "I remember sending him our shoes, our jerseys, our spandex so he could get every detail in how we wanted to display Nebraska Volleyball. With the dig. With the set. And the hit. Like the progression. That was significant. It could have been just a setter, but certainly it takes more than just a setter to make Nebraska Volleyball."

Noth in many ways did more than anyone to set up Nebraska Volleyball for decades of success. Husker fan Kari Beckenhauer said it's hard to measure Noth's contributions to the program. "Her impact is beyond words. She remains one of the pillars of the program, along with Doctor Hibner, Terry Pettit, and John Cook."

Being an Olympian was just one of many 1988 highlights for Noth. Her No. 11 Husker jersey was retired—a first for women's athletics at Nebraska—and she joined Pettit as an assistant coach. From 1988 to 1998 she helped the Huskers make five final fours and win one National Championship.

"The exciting part for me was coming back and being Terry's assistant and seeing the growth. Seeing the statue made. Getting new locker rooms. Still trying to maintain some of the venue that we had in the past. So that was really neat to intertwine that and be involved in that."

Fast forward to 2022, and Noth was enjoying life with her spouse, Eldonna, and their family in Madison, Wisconsin. Volleyball is still very much a part of her life, as she continues to train setters for two programs: Capital Academy in Madison and Northern Lights in Minnesota. What does Noth think of the Nebraska Volleyball program and the perks of being a player in 2022? "I think they're a little spoiled now," she said with a smile, "but that's just my opinion."

One of those recent stars is a setter named Kennedi Orr, who was trained by Noth at Northern Lights before joining the Huskers in 2021. Noth didn't do a lot of NU sales work with Orr. Actually, according to Orr, she didn't do any. "No, she didn't. The only thing she actually said to me when I committed was 'Did you know I went there?'"

Of course, Orr did know that bit of history. "She didn't talk a lot about it. I think she was pretty humble."

When working with her young setters, Noth says "Let's dream big. Where do you see yourself in five years?'" And when a standout volleyball player such as Orr dreams big, Nebraska usually enters the vision. "I loved the culture of Nebraska and loved the girls I was going to go here with," Orr said. "I see Cathy here on the wall every day, and I am like, 'Oh my gosh, I can't believe it.' I feel like when you are younger, you don't really realize what an impact older players had on a program, and I think coming here and seeing her name on the All-American wall every day is so cool, and reminds me of that time when I got to train with her.

"She's a pretty tough woman, but it's not tough in a sense like negativity. It's about being positive and sticking with yourself, and grinding and loving the grind, and I think that applies to everything in life. I think it was so cool that I got to train with her."

Orr, who redshirted in 2021, provides the Huskers with the potential of another great setter and another reason for Noth to visit Lincoln. "It's so fun to go back, especially when I'm with the team from 1996 or 1995 for the National Championship [celebration], and it just all comes back to you, everything you've gone through, and then as I see the Huskers in the present time, it's the same thing. You know a different venue, but knowing the drive and the passion and what Nebraska Volleyball stands for, I still feel that when I see them."

She came back in 2021 as a Hall of Famer, joining Pettit and Larson as new inductees into the University of Nebraska Athletic Hall of Fame. Husker radio voice John Baylor, one of her biggest fans, said he would have been lost without her support and the program wouldn't be what it is today without Cathy Noth. "So much of Nebraska Volleyball's success rests on her shoulders."

# 6

## Bertrand

While it's true that the small number of village occupants is a key factor, there has never been a lot of crime in Bertrand, Nebraska (pop. 750). In fact, Bob Dahlgren will tell you that it got so bad, or good, actually, that they fired Bertrand's only police officer because there was so little for him to do. "There was a village policeman until the mid-eighties, when we decided we didn't really need a policeman because they were just bored because there was nothing for them to do except zoning things, like people not mowing their lawn."

There is not much crime in Bertrand to this day. Still, some joke that the Dahlgren family was robbed when Karen came to Lincoln without a scholarship, a situation that was eventually corrected. A Bertrand high school valedictorian and Hall of Fame bargain who took one for the team a time or two on her way to becoming one of the sport's all-time greats.

The steal and the slide. That's the story of Karen Dahlgren (Schonewise), with the Schonewise name adding to the Big Red beauty of it all. It's more than fitting that Karen grew up in a spot located on the highest land between the Platte and Republican Rivers. Few Huskers have been able to tower over the net like Dahlgren did, and her name is still high up there in the record books, too.

She is grateful for the years that shaped her success. Here is the early part of her story, in her words:

A great childhood. I loved it very much. We lived half a block from the school. When you are a Class c or d school, everything in the community revolves around school, so I grew up playing all sports—volleyball, basketball, track, softball in the summers, and really enjoyed childhood. Track was probably the first sport that I really got involved in, in elementary school; did some AAU track meets, high jump, those kinds of things. My dad made a high-jump pit with standards and a bar with a large net containing foam pieces for the mat. He also made some hurdles when I got to high school. I worked part-time at the Bertrand Cafe the summer after my seventh grade year and full-time in the summers at the Bank of Bertrand from eighth grade through college. Also did some babysitting.

I went to a volleyball camp in Lincoln the summer before my senior year. Terry started recruiting me pretty hard then. He wanted me to play club volleyball. I had never played club volleyball. So we did drive to Lincoln, and I made a club team. The problem for me was they did everything on the weekends. And I had already committed to all my high school events. In addition to all the sports, I was a cheerleader, I was in choir, all of the other activities, and I had already made commitments to those things.

Terry still recruited me. He wanted me to walk on. For me it came down to Nebraska and Kearney State. I guess I had the thought at the time that I could try it in Lincoln and if things didn't work out at that level, I could probably always come back to Kearney State, since it was a smaller school and I would have actually had the opportunity to play multiple sports there. But I wanted to give it a shot and see if I could make it at the highest level. I got a partial scholarship after my first year. I was not on full scholarship until my senior year, so I like to tell Terry I was probably the best deal he ever got.

Mary Buysse was the setter when I first came in. I really enjoyed playing with "Bice." Only about 5-6. She only played back row. We ran a six-two at the time. Really enjoyed playing with her. Really competitive. Feisty. Cathy Noth was the other setter in that system. Also, obviously a great player. A lot of fun.

One of the most defining things for me was my first year I redshirted, so I literally shagged balls all fall. On occasion I might get in the last minute or two of a drill, but truly just shagged balls all fall. And in the spring, the rules were such that I was allowed to play on an alumni team during the USVBA spring season, and bless their hearts, the alums took me in, and I got to play a lot and it really helped my development. I got to play with Lori Melcher Hunter and Reba Govier and Nancy Grant Colson and Gwen Egbert. Just a really great experience to play with the alums.

Later, a great experience for those alums to say that they got to play with Dahlgren. She did not, however, win over too many teammates with her serving skills as a young Husker. She had a hard time getting the ball over the net and in play, and since Pettit had expectations about such things, that meant more running for the team. "I struggled with that," she said, laughing, "especially early on."

So really it was just another way she worked her fellow Huskers into shape. That is real leadership. But her struggles were few, and she did become a better server and a great leader. Noth said it was fun to watch Pettit and Dahlgren join forces to make Karen a star and one of the top middle blockers in the land. "This is what Terry does so well," Noth said. "Terry works toward your strengths. Terry knew that she was a jumper, and to run that slide was so much fun. To me the adjustment of setting it wasn't that hard. It was just the amazement of Karen getting it right away. That's talent. Terry talks about talent and skill. That's talent. The skill came from getting the elbow up high and swinging through the ball. That's skill. But she had the talent."

The slide became a big deal at Nebraska and all over the country. "She was that amazing slide attacker, came around the back side and just popped and really, I feel like one of the first people to really master that," said teammate Kathi DeBoer (Wieskamp). "It's now more common. You see that all the time. She was so good at it, so quick, moved so well along the net."

Often Dahlgren's key partner on the play was setter Tisha Delaney. "Tisha's posture at the net was maybe different than any other setter that I had," Pettit said. "Most setters tended to square up to the left front hitter. Tisha tended to have her hips more oriented toward left back. And she was very consistent from there, and particularly she could set the slide from that position. The slide was so effective. You could tell the other team you were going to run it but they couldn't do anything about it." At that time they didn't know how to defend it. "The issue was that the slide hitter, because she was leaping off one foot, leaves the floor much faster than the blocker, and you have to understand that and have trained for that. Even today I would say the slide probably is the highest percentage attack in women's volleyball."

It's a play that was also key to the arsenal of Husker star Lauren Stivrins some thirty-five years later. And, wouldn't you know, through the 2021 season Dahlgren (.386) and Stivrins (.378) were third and fourth on the Husker career charts for hitting percentage. One difference was that Stivrins, thanks to Name, Image, and Likeness, was able to make a few bucks on "Rise and Slide" T-shirts created during her final season. That was not a thing when Dahlgren was doing her thing.

Delaney said it was something to behold. "First of all, her athleticism. I mean, she glided on the court. She was like a dancer. She glided. And yet, the power. How do you have this beautiful dichotomy of grace and fierce power? It was just a thing of beauty."

Dahlgren, at six feet, won over fans and teammates with the slide and a quiet command that made her one of the program's all-time greats. Not just on the court but in the classroom as well. She was a two-time All-American and a three-time Academic All-American. In 1986 she was the Honda Award winner as the top player in the country. After her playing days Karen did quite a bit of coaching at various levels, including from 1988 to 1997 at the University of Kansas, the last four years as head coach with a record of 34-86.

"Didn't have a ton of success when I was coaching there," she said. "I was an assistant for a long time, then I took the head job, and then a year later we went from the Big Eight to the Big 12, so it became even more challenging at that point. Just didn't feel like I had quite enough time to develop the things I wanted to develop there. Loved the university. I came from Nebraska, where we won all the time, to Kansas, where we didn't win a whole lot. Losing gives you a lot more opportunity to find out about your character and how you handle things and battle through things and the ability to stay positive and stay focused on the right things."

It didn't work out at KU, but DeBoer said Dahlgren was a great teammate and an amazing leader. Not a rah-rah in-your-face leader. An encourager. "On the court she really led by example, with her great work ethic, very intense and focused as a player. I never really saw her get rattled."

Not all of her Jayhawk stories were downers. There was this University of Kansas offensive lineman named Quintin

Schonewise, and well . . . you might see where this is going. "Quintin had asked his sister Enid to set him up with one of her teammates," Dahlgren said, referring to Husker teammate Enid Schonewise. "She picked me, thinking we might be a good fit and set us up on a blind date. I met him in the hallway of the Coliseum after a spring volleyball tournament and my first impression was that he was a tall, handsome man with a gentle handshake. He told me later that people always expected a firm or even bone-crushing handshake from offensive linemen, so he usually did the opposite. It certainly made an impression on me. We had a long-distance relationship, as we never lived in the same state the entire time we dated. Enid chose well—we've been married over thirty years."

Their daughters, Lillian and Olivia, were standout volleyball players at Papillion South High School near Omaha. Their head coach was Gwen Egbert. Their school principal was Enid Schonewise. Husker family ties everywhere.

At the end of the 2021 season Dahlgren still held school records for most blocks in a single match with 18 (against U.S. International in 1984) and she was No. 5 on the all-time chart for career blocks with 558. Dahlgren's No. 13 was retired by the Huskers in 1988, and in 2017 she became a Husker Hall of Famer. "Very surreal," she said. "Pretty exciting. John Cook was actually the one who made the call to tell me, so that was pretty cool."

Mr. Dream Big himself. Pretty cool, yep. Like Dahlgren, a walk-on from the mostly crime-free Village of Bertrand, Nebraska. "You have to dream big," she said. "You just don't know what you can achieve until you dream those big dreams."

# How the West Was Warned

As Karen Dahlgren knows better than anyone, the story of the 1986 season and the program's first trip to the Final Four is one that will knock you right in the kisser. Three seniors who remained best friends for all time led the Huskers to the NCAA Championship match that season, but it was a rough road at the outset.

A key staff member at the time was assistant coach Jay Potter, who joined the staff in 1984 after getting the volleyball program going at Colorado Christian in Denver. Pettit said Potter was a great addition to the team, not just another mind in the mix. He also had some serious southpaw game as a player. "Jay Potter was left-handed," Pettit said, "and so when we needed to replicate a strong left-handed attacker on the other team, he would be on the court. You used whatever resources you had."

Potter, like Cook, was a California native who will always be grateful for the chance to be part of Pettit's program. "I had very little coaching experience, really. For Terry to take me on at a Division I school, I consider myself pretty fortunate," Potter said. "Everything at that level was a bigger deal, a much bigger deal for me. The whole time there was really a treat for me, and I really enjoyed it. I learned how to coach from Terry Pettit and think like a coach instead of thinking like a player. It shaped me as a coach, really, and I've considered Terry as my mentor ever since.

"Terry was on a mission. He was extremely serious and focused, and one of the best things I learned from him is to be a successful coach you must be consistent with the level of your expectations. You can't waver on those." In the spring after the 1985 season, when the No. 6–ranked Huskers lost to No. 3 USC at home in a regional final, Pettit and Potter didn't see a lot of fire. They knew they had a talented crew, but something was missing in the spark department. The potential and the expectations were not aligned.

"Things were going in a direction that we weren't used to as coaches," Potter said. "Terry said, 'We've got to do something to snap this team out of it.' Terry said, 'Jay I want you to hit Karen Dahlgren in the face with the ball at practice today.'" What? Potter's response was: "She's the hardest-working kid I've ever coached. I can't do that."

They went back and forth about it for quite a while before Potter agreed to do it, under one condition: that Pettit and Potter would make sure Dahlgren knew what was coming. She did, and she basically said, "Okay, whatever it takes." "Karen is probably the best leader I've ever had," Potter said. "She understood it. She understood that what she did mattered and that every single thing she did, on and off the court, was important."

In the pit drill, Potter said, the players would have to dig ten balls to get out of the drill, and the coach would make it really hard. One on one, coach against player. "I would hit balls down in front of her, just out of her reach. She could touch them but not dig them. She kept moving closer and closer to me, and then I hit one deep and hit her right in the face. She looked at me for an instant with this, 'I wish you didn't have to do that' look, and then she puts her arms out and her fists in front of her and she goes 'Come on!' The whole team is circling around, and their faces drop, and they knew right then, there are no excuses at all. That turned the team around. That was the spring season right before we went to the Final Four. That was the first team that went to the Final Four. It changed the whole program around, that one single thing. Pettit understood Karen much better than I did at that time. He knew that she would use it to help the team. Afterward I was more in awe of Karen than ever before. That's a story I've used over the years many times. When players want to start making excuses, I'm like, 'This is what a leader does.'"

Whatever-it-takes leadership. "I know that Jay really struggled with that method to fire up the team," Dahlgren said. "He let me know right before practice what he had been instructed to do, and I really appreciated the heads up. Jay was a great balance for Terry. Jay has such a great personality and kept things fun and light for us."

Another Small Town Nebraska leader was starting to emerge at the time. Enid Schonewise, a 6-foot-1 outside hitter from Beatrice. "Enid, her first two years, was kind of in the background," Potter said. "I think she struggled some with the higher level and the expectations and not playing as much as she was used to playing. But then in the spring of her sophomore year, spring season, in a club tournament, she had 25 kills, and we were like, 'What just happened?' Then the spring season's over, and she comes back for her junior year and continues to play like that and starts to lead. Totally unexpected. Our program that year could not have been that successful without her making that change."

Schonewise recalled feeling "a new sense of confidence" in 1986. "I remember thinking, 'Give me the ball' when we were in a really tough jam." The Huskers found themselves in a bit of a jam right out of the gate in the fall. Senior setter Tisha Delaney (Vandermore) was suspended for three matches after her photo appeared in a Women of Nebraska calendar, a fundraiser for Mothers Against Drunk Driving. Jon Kelley, who was part of the football and track-and-field programs, was suspended for part of the track season for appearing in the men's version of the calendar. The punishment for Delaney was viewed by many to be a little harsh considering that it was not an NCAA violation, but she sat anyway. "I was so naïve," Delaney said. "I just accepted the ruling."

The team had a young star who filled in for Delaney in the opening matches, a future Olympian no less: Lori Endicott (Vandersnick). But without their starting setter, the Huskers lost their first match, at home, against Nebraska-Omaha, coached by none other than former Husker Janice Kruger. Not exactly what anyone expected from the No. 3–ranked team in the nation.

The match at the Coliseum went five sets, with UNO winning the fifth 15–13. A year before, the Huskers had smoked the Omaha crew in three sets, so the 1986 upset was a big deal, especially for Kruger, who said she didn't feel like the Huskers respected her team on that day. Sort of like how UNL felt when they faced teams from the West Coast.

Kruger recalled a conversation with Pettit before the match about Nebraska possibly providing some sort of guarantee for the Omaha visitors—a few bucks for meals or something like that. She said Pettit only promised a guarantee of a quick Husker victory. Pettit doesn't remember that conversation, but he did say that after Nebraska went up 2–1 in the match, he wanted to get a lot of players in the mix and on the floor. He said it was not for a lack of respect for the opponent. He tipped his cap to Kruger's crew. "It was more a matter of UNO playing really well, particularly in the fifth set."

Schonewise recalled some lineup chaos in the match, mainly because Delaney was not available. "That certainly affected us. It was just a weird start," she said. "It was in the Coliseum, 100 degrees, with no air conditioning, at least that's how I remember it. It was a long match. That was a frustrating way to start."

Schonewise said they couldn't wait to hit reset with Delaney—the "Irish Setter"—back on the court. "It must've been something, because we had a great season once Tisha got back on the roster."

Delaney came to Nebraska from Herculaneum High School and Jefferson College, both about 40 miles south of St. Louis. She was a JUCO All-American with offers from several big schools, including Missouri and Minnesota, but she quickly realized Lincoln was the place for her. "When I took my recruiting trip to Nebraska, you could just tell," she said. "When I went there, it just connected, and I knew that's where I belonged. So when I sat down with Coach Pettit, he told me I could go to Mizzou and likely be an All-American, but the question is, 'Do you want to win a championship?' He asked me, 'Do you want to be an All-American and make history? That was it. I was ready to sign."

Pettit and Noth were key mentors in her development. "What he was brilliant at was recognizing personalities. He knew how to get the most out of each individual personality. I'd say to this day, in the business world, if people could do that, they could understand that you just can't have a flat way to deal with people, to get the best out of them," Delaney said. "Cathy Noth was instrumental in my success because she trained me. She and I would work separately. And she would mentor me. And obviously, she went on to play in the Olympics. What made me respect her the most was the time that she would give me off the court, because she wanted the program to be successful and she knew I was the one coming in to replace her."

Delaney and Endicott were both grateful for the short-lived Host Parent program, which gave Huskers from other states a Lincoln family to connect with to ease any potential homesick issues. Delaney, who was matched with Jack and Vicki Highstreet, said the program was a hug beyond compare. "It truly was so important in my transition as a transfer. It's lonely. You know no one. Even your surroundings, coaching staff, and teammates are 'strangers.' Jack and Vicki Highstreet were such wonderful influences in my life. They were so supportive, opening their hearts and home to me. It was such a comfort to go to their house and have a home-cooked meal, do laundry, spend quality time with their daughters, Jennifer and Andrea, and have a safe place. I attribute the safety and support network they provided as part of the reason for my growth, development, and success.

"I'm uncertain if this was the original intent of the program or simply a side benefit, but the program allowed me to see firsthand what unselfishness and kindness by 'strangers' looks like. The Highstreet family was a great role model. When I graduated I carried with me their lesson to show grace to those I don't know well. For that, I'm forever grateful. It takes a village."

Kari and Tom Beckenhauer were part of that village for Endicott, who came to Lincoln from Springfield, Missouri. "Leaving home at eighteen was a difficult transition for me, not just in volleyball but in school as well," Endicott said. "Of course, I loved my time with the team and coaches, but I missed home and the comfort that my parents brought me mentally and emotionally. The Host Parent program allowed players like me to have a relaxed place to take a break from the volleyball and college world and lessen some of the stress that I felt. Something as simple as a home-cooked meal, easy conversation, or simply watching a TV show on a comfy couch could ease some of that pressure. I needed that in order to help me transition from a high school student athlete into a college one, especially at one of the top programs in the country. I'm so appreciative to Tom and Kari. Their support brought a feeling of solace that I sometimes desperately needed."

The program only lasted a couple of years due to NCAA rules concerns, but Lori and the Beckenhauers have stayed in touch. Kari and Tom were in Atlanta to see Endicott compete as an Olympian in 1996. "People at other schools were abusing the program by giving athletes, cars, money, jobs, etc.," Kari said. "There were many great things about the Host Parent program, but mainly it gave the student-athlete some place to be away from UNL and their sport. They could have a taste of home while being away from home. And if they didn't know where to get a flat tire fixed, you could give them guidance on where to go, for example. You were limited to letting them have a soda or something very small when they visited your house. No palatial meals, no taking them out to eat or to the movies, etc. Athletes could decompress a bit by being with their host families."

The 1986 Huskers could have been considered a young team, but they had some big-time leadership at the top. Delaney, Dahlgren, and Schonewise were the captains. All seniors. There was one junior, Kathi DeBoer, and two sophomores, Endicott and Angie Millikin. The rest were freshmen: Carla Baker, Linda Barsness, Jackie Cook, Michelle Davis, DeLisa DeBolt, Susie Hansen, Barbie Young, and redshirt Virginia Stahr.

Everyone had a role, but the three seniors led the way. DeBoer, Endicott, Young, and Millikin are also often mentioned as key contributors as underclassmen that season. "The pressure they had," Delaney said. "Like Barbie Young, to come in and serve match point in games." Probably make a good doctor, that Barbie Young.

Schonewise said the team had a lot of fun off the court and that contributed to their success on it. "There were several of us on that team that liked to push boundaries a little bit, that were a little spicy. I think you have to have some of that on a team, and I think we had a lot of fun on and off the court. We liked to have fun together. We liked to be a little ornery together."

Like the time Tisha snuck one of her aunt's famous cheesecakes, made fresh in Festus, and they just pigged out on the bus. Of course, the bus that didn't have Coach Pettit on board. "When we traveled to Mizzou we had two buses at the time, they were Greyhound buses, which was nice, but we had two buses, and Coach Pettit was on one coming back, and a cluster of us were all on the other, and my aunt wanted to bring me our favorite cheesecake. Of course, when you are in the program, you're supposed to be eating healthy. So we all snuck the cheesecake on the opposite bus as Pettit. And all of us were in there digging into the cheesecake on the ride home, which is just terrible."

After the loss to Omaha, the Huskers won 22 of their next 25 matches and cruised to another Big Eight title with a 10-0 conference record. At that point Nebraska had not lost a Big Eight match in five years. The Huskers were 52-0 in league play from 1983 to 1987.

The team was rolling with another superstar in the making in Endicott, a 5-foot-9 right-side attacker at the time. "The first word that comes to mind when I remember her from that period in time is 'explosive,'" Delaney said. "For her height she could jump out of the gym."

While the Huskers were dominating the Big Eight, they were still trying to prove they could play with Texas and the top teams out west, including perennial power Hawaii, which lost a match in Lincoln in 1985. That was a good sign for the midwesterners, and so was a win over UCLA in a tournament near the end of the 1986 season. That event was hosted by No. 2 Pacific, a mighty bunch at that time.

Led by Elaina Oden, one of the all-time greats at middle blocker, Pacific beat Nebraska in three in that same tournament, but the No. 6 Huskers then won five matches in a row on their way to a regional final against ninth-ranked Illinois at the Bob Devaney Sports Center, a newer facility on campus used for basketball and bigger events. "It was just a different environment," Schonewise said, "and it felt special."

The match wasn't even close: 15–9, 15–8, 15–3. A piece of cake, compared to the five-setter they won against Penn State in the Regional Semifinal. Nebraska was going to the Final Four. "It was freaking amazing," Schonewise said. "It was overwhelming. It was so exciting. I just remember being on cloud nine. It was the best feeling ever."

DeBoer remembers great hoopla about the accomplishment at home but little more than polite applause in Stockton, California, when the team arrived for the National Semifinals. "I remember this article in the [Omaha] paper, and it's a volleyball in the middle. It's just kind of a cartoon character and had a volleyball in the middle, a football on one side, and a basketball. And the volleyball was throwing elbows and saying, 'Move over boys.' And when we were out there, the people were super nice, but it was kind of like 'Great, you made it, but we do this all the time.' From that perspective I think we shocked a lot of people because it had been all West Coast teams. That's just who it had been. I think it kind of opened their eyes that there were good things happening in the Midwest and in Nebraska."

Dahlgren knew what a monumental bar the program had reached. "Making the first Final Four was both exhilarating and a relief. We felt we should have made it the previous year, but we played poorly in the regional final, so I definitely felt the pressure. I remember Pettit coming into the locker room after we won, and it was such an overwhelming moment of joy. He and I had been there the longest, as the program had had different assistant coaches during my years and I had redshirted, so I was in my fifth year. My freshman year I had played on a USVBA team with former players, so I also felt a responsibility to the alums. It was truly a time of triumph and satisfaction to make that first Final Four, surpassed only by the win against Stanford in the semifinals."

Yes, about that win over the Cardinal in the semifinals. Another big deal for the program. The Huskers advanced to the championship by beating No. 11 Stanford in four: 7–15, 15–2, 15–10, 15–10. "Perhaps Stanford was just loose and confident, but we felt they did not respect us when they took the floor and throughout warm-ups," Delaney said. "Their experience at the Final Four showed early in the match, but we settled down in the second and got into our rhythm. We were looking forward to that Stanford match. We knew we had the stronger team."

Millikin was a big part of the semifinal win, with 11 kills and 18 digs. "She stabilized us," Pettit said. Schonewise led the Huskers with 15 kills. Team hitting numbers were lopsided— Nebraska .258, Stanford .089. "I distinctly remember feeling strength in knowing we just beat ourselves that first game," Delaney said. "That meant we could make changes and still win the match. That is exactly what we did. We settled in, refocused, and believed in each other. I had the privilege and benefit of playing with the best outside and middle hitters in the country. I knew that and after that match the rest of the country knew it as well."

That Husker bunch was the first team outside of California or Hawaii to make the NCAA championship match in women's volleyball. But that was where the beach fun ended. Pacific swept through the Final Four—knocking off Texas first and then Nebraska (15–12, 15–4, 15–4)—for its second straight national title. But what a season it had been for the Huskers.

NU set an NCAA record at the time with a .331 hitting percentage. Dahlgren, Delaney, and Schonewise were all honored as All-Americans while becoming best buddies forever. "We still keep a text chain," Delaney said. "We still talk. We still see each other. They came to my daughter's wedding [in North Carolina]. This is what Nebraska Volleyball is. It's not just at the time." But what a time that was. "We made it further than any Nebraska team in history."

# Firth

# 8

Kathi DeBoer was a big part of that historic 1986 run, and like Karen Dahlgren and so many others, she was from Small Town, Nebraska. "I loved playing with Kathi," said Dahlgren. "She was such a great teammate—sweet and genuine off the court, but a tireless worker and competitive on the court."

DeBoer grew up on a dairy farm in Firth (population 600) and attended Norris High School, which later produced another Husker star, Megan Korver (1996–98). Firth is about 25 miles south of Lincoln. A short trip to the University of Nebraska. But short doesn't mean easy. We will let Kathi share all of that:

> Farm life. Bottle feeding calves each day, helping with chores both on the farm and in the home. Dairy farm parents (Robert and Virginia). We milked twice a day, and so we were included in those farm chores as well, and having to get up for school on our own, and my mother would get in from milking and prepare a breakfast for us before we went to school, as that was required to have breakfast before we went to school in the morning. Always outdoors and doing things, playing outdoors, exploring, and not a lot of TV. Summers we had a big garden and so I helped

with all of that and often would ride in the combine or on the tractor with my dad and grandfather.

After school it was time for milking again and so we took care of feeding the baby calves and other jobs, usually did a few things outside (ride bikes, shoot baskets, gardening) and then went in to do homework until suppertime. Life was pretty much school, work, and family. I am one of four kids, so I always had siblings around as well. Work ethic was taught. That is something I give credit to my family for.

My high school coach at Norris was Karen Frazee, a pentathlete from NU. I came in as a freshman, and it was her first year out of college. She really got you involved. She really understood the collegiate level. Former Husker Jan Zink was also influential. I played in the very first high school all-star game in 1984. Myron Oehlerking was my coach. Sandi Genrich was the other coach. Steve Morgan, Phyllis Rice, Deb Graffington, Nancy Grant Colson were all involved. That was when club volleyball was just once every two or three months and you got together for a tournament or whatever. Nancy started that connection when I was really young. I got connected to Nebraska Volleyball in high school.

The year before I committed, they played in an NCAA regional final. I just remember them playing in that and that it was a big deal. You had people getting connected to the program. That's when it was really building. As soon as they offered, then it was done.

DeBoer was a 5-foot-11 outside hitter. When she started out as a Husker, DeBoer said Dahlgren was a key mentor, but she mentioned Annie Adamczak as a role model as well. "She was tough and she held people accountable."

Adamczak was a 5-foot-10 middle blocker from Moose

Lake, Minnesota. She came to Nebraska in part for the chance to play two sports—basketball and volleyball. She was Minnesota's Ms. Basketball in high school. Nebraska was one of only a couple of big schools that were going to give her that multisport chance.

Potter has a favorite story about Annie. "She played some basketball at Nebraska, but through that process she realized she was a volleyball player. After her junior season of volleyball Pettit said she could play basketball. She came back before the end of our spring season in 1985, and at the second practice back she announced in the middle of practice out loud, 'I'm going to be an All-American next year. I'm going to be a First Team All-American.' Silence in the gym. Nobody says anything. Terry and I look at each other. She's the fourth-best hitter on the team. She's probably overall the fourth-best player on the team. Then practice is over and as the door is closing, Terry says, 'Can you believe Adamczak?'

"Well, Annie Adamczak changed how she ate, how she drank, how she slept, how she thought. She changed everything to reach that goal, and by golly, she was a First Team All-American that next year. I learned a lesson. You can never tell a kid she can't do something."

From Adamczak and Dahlgren and the other veterans, DeBoer got a primer on the importance of hard work and accountability. She said Cathy Noth and Julie Hermann were also strong teachers on the court. From Pettit she learned more about the thought process that makes a champion. "He's so cerebral. Analyze. Process. Think things through. When I was a freshman, the only freshman who traveled, we used to drive a lot. So guess who gets to ride with the coach? You just kind of got used to it. Even when I listen to him speak now, in his books, it's like his voice in my head. I enjoyed playing for him. Thinking things through. Analyzing for the good of the cause."

As a junior DeBoer hit .322 with 421 kills, including 30 in the 1986 Regional Semifinal against Penn State. She excelled on offense and defense as a senior, leading the Huskers with 529 kills and 372 digs. After her playing days, DeBoer said Pettit lined it up so she and Noth would coach a club team with players from all over the state. "We had girls driving in four hours from Ogallala every weekend to practice. We practiced at Lincoln Christian [High School]. They drove in from Ogallala with their parents. Janet Kruse's younger sister, Jodi, played for us. Allison Weston and others. It truly was the best in the state coming together. It kept growing, and club kept growing. It just exploded."

DeBoer has been in the game in one way or another ever since, as a coach at Lincoln Southeast High School for fifteen years and then also the school's athletic director. And for more than twenty-five years she has been part of the Nebraska Public Media (formerly NET) coverage of Nebraska Volleyball, which is a big part of the state-treasure part of the story. "They asked me to [cover] a summer all-star game, and they said if it goes well, we might be interested in having you do a Nebraska game. So that's kind of how it started. Steve Alvis and Jim Carmichael were the guys I first worked with. Bill Doleman was my partner, and Kevin Kugler was kind of his backup, and then I worked with Kevin for a lot of years.

"I was in Ogallala for a retreat in 2019, and we stopped in this small little town to look at a historic building, and you called this lady, and she came to tell you the history of this little church. Anyway, she started talking and she said, 'I know who you are. Are you Kathi Wieskamp? We never miss a game out here. We love it.' That's the feeling. She said we never get to come to games, so we don't miss any of them out here. That's our opportunity. I go to my mother-in-law's for a Christmas party, and there's eighty-some people there, and guess what? The games are on, and nobody's talking about anything but the game and what's going on. They're hooked. And once people go once [to a match], they're hooked."

Kathi gives all the credit in the world to Pettit and Cook and all they have done to promote volleyball in Nebraska towns big and small, while providing guidance to high school coaches from Scottsbluff to Omaha. "I do think we have great coaches out there. Coaches who have chosen to be students of the game. I think Coach Pettit started that. He's a sharer. I think Coach Cook's the same way. No secrets. I definitely believe Nebraska Volleyball opens doors. People can see that you can be great and you can do great things for kids and kids can go on to do great things."

Like Kathi. In 2013 Wieskamp was named director of athletics and activities for Lincoln Public Schools, shortly after being named athletic director of the year for her work at Lincoln Southeast. She retired in June 2022 with a strong record of doing her part to make sure young people have the same chances she had while growing up on that dairy farm in Firth, Nebraska. "We're giving kids opportunities."

# 9

# Ogallala

It's a long way from Firth and Lincoln, but for a land of volleyball opportunity in Nebraska, it's hard to top Ogallala and the doors opened there by Steve Morgan. Diane Schroeder (Mendenhall). Angie Millikin (Goodgame). Angie Oxley (Behrens). All three were Ogallala High School Indians who excelled at the University of Nebraska in one way or another. All because of what the Schroeder family and Morgan created in a town of about 4,500 located where the pan meets the handle in western Nebraska.

"Coach Morgan was the reason I fell in love with the game of volleyball," Oxley said. Millikin laughed when talking about how she was at first a little frightened by Steve. "We were scared to death of the guy because he was a large man with a big old mustache and lots of hair and you did what Mr. Morgan said," she said. "He carried himself in a big old way with a big deep voice." But, Millikin adds, "he's an unbelievable motivator. My mom wanted me to be on the drill team but I didn't think that was a very good idea. I liked the volleyball program better once I peeked in the gym and saw what they were doing."

Morgan said it was Millikin's mad dog spirit that sparked much of his program's success. "Let's just say she was kind of the wild one, in a good way," he said. "Had to kind of keep tabs on her a little. When we would go out of town for a club tournament or whatever, the first thing on my mind was, okay, where's Angie? But talk about pulling through as far as being an athlete. What she did to help this program get going was second to none."

Ogallala was a former Pony Express stop, a good four hours west of Lincoln, but it is very close to the heart of the story, and no one know tells it better than Ogallala High graduate Todd von Kampen. With his permission, here is a large excerpt of a story Todd wrote in 2019 for the *North Platte Telegraph*.

No photograph would be complete without the instrument of Steve Morgan's coaching success. Jingling his keys, the 72-year-old legend unlocked an Ogallala Auditorium closet door to find a volleyball for a newspaper picture one day in the spring of 2019. North and south, concrete-anchored bleachers rose to the ceiling. The west end held the stage where the Ogallala High School pep band revved up one capacity crowd after another to a fever pitch. The young women Morgan coached did the rest, diving for saves or soaring to pound the ball into the wooden floor of "the Aud."

The roots of volleyball in Nebraska, a statewide passion now second only to Husker football, were sunk in many towns over many decades. This is the story of one such town, one where volleyball still was thriving proudly as Morgan stepped down that spring after 45 years as Ogallala coach. Even Morgan will tell you, however, that Ogallala's volleyball story doesn't start at "the Aud" or even with him. It starts on a concrete slab near a church.

The first St. Paul Lutheran School and its original outdoor court are both long gone. The Missouri Synod congregation built its current school and fellowship hall, featuring a carpeted court, where it stood 40 years ago. Next to that concrete slab stood a small white house where two of the unsung parents of Ogallala volleyball once lived.

Lee Schroeder, a pastor's son, began teaching at St. Paul's in 1960 and became principal a year later. He and his wife, Doris, spent their first years with daughters Pam, Diane and Jennie in that little white house. The concrete slab was their playground and their backyard. And that's where volleyball in Ogallala was born. "At recess, whatever was in season, we played," said Diane Schroeder, the middle daughter. "There was no separation as far as girls and boys. We all played together."

Most Nebraskans know her as Diane Mendenhall, University of Nebraska director of volleyball operations from 2000 to 2006. The court was built for basketball, and the fence around the Schroeders' house made for a great outfield wall for kickball. But sometime in the mid-1960s, Lee Schroeder put up a portable volleyball net hanging from steel poles and anchored with concrete-filled tires. Why did he introduce volleyball?

Pam Schroeder traces that to her mother—one of uncounted hundreds of Nebraska women who planted what current Husker Coach John Cook calls volleyball's "hidden DNA." Organized girls volleyball teams spread across Nebraska's smaller high schools starting in the 1920s—a time when school administrators were banning full-court girls basketball, labeling it too dangerous. But girls volleyball flourished—and it received a further boost when Peru State College founded a state high school tournament in 1946.

More than 150 Nebraska schools were playing volleyball by the late 1950s. The group included Doris Schroeder's hometown of Waco. That's where she played volleyball and softball. It's also where she met a Missouri boy named Lee. "My dad was an athlete, so he had the background," said the oldest daughter, Pam Schroeder. "My mom had an athletic spirit. They had a love of sport."

Ogallala wasn't part of Nebraska's early volleyball wave. But when its high school added the sport in 1972, St. Paul's alumnae already knew and loved volleyball. That group included the two daughters of the Rev. Juraine Hornig, who became St. Paul's pastor in 1969 and lived across West Third Street from the court. In the winters, Diane said, "I remember playing [volleyball] with mittens on." On warmer days, Hornig would hang around the concrete court while Lee Schroeder, who retired as principal in 1994 and died in 2015, joined in his pupils' spirited matches using that portable volleyball net. Then Steve Morgan came back from the service.

He knew nothing about volleyball before he left, he says. The small-school volleyball movement that initially missed Ogallala also missed Mitchell, next door to Scottsbluff, where Morgan graduated from high school in 1964. Nor did he pick up the game at Kearney State College (today's University of Nebraska at Kearney), from which Morgan received his teaching degree in 1968. He first taught elementary P.E. in Ogallala's public schools until 1971, when the U.S. Army drafted him. Morgan was assigned to a military police unit at Fort Leonard Wood in Missouri—where a member of his unit had recently been cut from the U.S. national men's volleyball team. When he heard that, Morgan said, "I told him I thought it was a sissy sport. And he said, 'Why don't you come over? We have a makeshift gym, and I'll teach you a few skills.' I fell in love with it."

Discharged in 1973, Morgan brought his new love back to Ogallala's public schools. They now had a high school volleyball team—though school board President Jim Ayres, then a high school math teacher, said administrators had added it without much enthusiasm. But Pam Schroeder, now a junior, and her old St. Paul's schoolmates eagerly embraced the new opportunity. "I remember watching the boys play my freshman and sophomore years and thinking, 'I want to be out there. I want to compete. Why can't I compete?'" she said. "I was a cheerleader, but that wasn't my thing."

She and Leah Hornig, the pastor's older daughter, showed up for founding coach Marci Tucker's first practice. So did St. Paul's classmates Marcia Adkins and Margie and Kathy Bauer. Ellen Kolste and Rita Knight had come up through the public schools. Tammy Berry, who had played in Arthur's schools, drove 37 miles south through the Sandhills to join the Indians.

That first Ogallala volleyball team won about half its matches. In 1973, with Brenda Van Newkirk taking over from Tucker, the Indians posted their first winning record but lost in the district semifinals. The next wave of St. Paul's players, led by Diane Schroeder and Leah Hornig's sister, Lois, would be joining the 1974 Indians as sophomores. Steve Morgan, meanwhile, had already started teaching volleyball to his P.E. pupils at West Fifth and Progress-West Ward schools.

At the latter—now the site of Ogallala's Kathleen Lute Public Library—he had his female pupils throw and "bump" a red rubber ball off the east wall. "That's all we had," Morgan said. "We didn't have a legal volleyball of any kind."

He had known junior high science teacher Dick Lungrin since both had attended Kearney State. Lungrin's wife, Carol, had been assistant coach for Van Newkirk, who didn't return for 1974. Carol was asked to take the job, Dick Lungrin said, but they both wanted Morgan to take over—if they could persuade athletic director Elwin Tophoj that a man could coach teenage girls without causing scandal. "We bought a 12-pack of beer and drove out to Elwin's place with Steve, and we sat down and had a two-hour conversation with Elwin and polished off the six-pack," he said.

Even before that, "we had a few drinks, and I think that's how I had enough guts to go over and ask for the job," Morgan recalled. Carol Lungrin agreed to remain as assistant and supervise the girls in the locker room. Morgan would enter only when they were ready to play.

In late August 1974, Morgan took the Ogallala Auditorium floor for his first practice. From the start, Diane Schroeder says, he focused relentlessly on fundamentals—and motivation.

He quickly debuted three-on-three scrimmages. With only half the usual six players per side, it put a premium on diving to keep the ball in play. It also showed which players had mastered the skills to anchor the Indians' starting lineup. That's where St. Paul's concrete court paid off, Diane Schroeder said. She and Lois Hornig needed little time to win their places alongside Leah Hornig, Margie Bauer, Berry, Barb Reimers and Susan Bailey. "The cool thing about St. Paul's was there's so many transferrable skills from volleyball to other sports. We were prepared so well," she said.

Meanwhile, Lee Schroeder had launched his school's first competitive volleyball team and encouraged St. Luke's Catholic School to start one. To the very end of his career, Morgan—a native Catholic who joined the St. Paul's congregation with his 1977 marriage—could count on a steady stream of players from his own church. His first team was both talented and unusually cohesive, he said. "They were a group. No one was left out." But Diane Schroeder said Morgan also knew how to bring out their best. "My memory of Coach Morgan is just psychological—believing that we had all this great talent and that we could win."

Morgan, who retired with a 984–217 record, won nearly 82 percent of his matches. He never came close to a losing season. His first Ogallala team posted a 15-3 record. But only a couple hundred people were seeing their matches—until one day in November 1974.

With relatively few Nebraska high schools yet playing volleyball, the Indians were the 32nd and smallest team in Class A. Its district included North Platte—already playing Ogallala at least twice a year—and Scottsbluff and Gering, Panhandle neighbors and rivals. When the four schools' coaches chose their district tournament site, Lungrin said, Scottsbluff and Gering canceled each other out. But NPHS Coach Linda Carlson, whose Bulldogs would win back-to-back Class A crowns in 1979 and 1980, sided with Morgan. Ogallala would host.

All three matches would be played the same day. Morgan's Indians won that morning, before their usual sparse crowd, to set up an evening match with Scottsbluff for a state tournament berth. Schroeder, the Hornig girls and their mates emerged from their locker room for warmups—to a huge Auditorium crowd. "We went out to the gym to warm up, and it was just packed and hot," Schroeder said. "It was an amazing atmosphere between the students and the community and the parents."

All that afternoon, Lungrin said, Ogallala's radio stations had been reminding the town that the volleyball team was playing for a trip to state. Though the cross-country team had won a Class B crown in 1972, the school had never won a team title in football, basketball or track. "That night, the whole damn town came to that game," Lungrin said. "We had people who were hungry for something."

The Indians played the match of their lives. The crowd roared on every point. With a full house, Ogallala enjoyed an intimidating home-court advantage. It was the night the town fell in love with volleyball. The match went the full three sets. Ogallala prevailed. The Indians were district champs in the program's third year. They traveled up the North Platte River the next week to Scottsbluff, host of the Nebraska School Activities Association's first state tournaments from 1972 to 1976.

Ogallala kept its fans' enthusiasm stoked with a first-round, three-set victory over Papillion. But semifinal opponent Lincoln East had future Husker Nancy Grant, whose left-handed serve proved difficult to stop, Schroeder said. The Spartans won in straight sets, then won the state crown. But Morgan's teams would never play before tiny home crowds again.

With Schroeder and Lois Hornig leading the way, Ogallala posted a 14-2 record in 1975. When Ayres would drive around town, he said, "you didn't see girls shooting baskets. You'd see them bumping volleyballs or hitting them against the house."

The Indians got used to sweaty conditions, noisy timeouts, football players leading cheers and Leo Ruhlman, chief cheerleader of the adults' Whompem-Stompem Booster Club, parading through the stands garishly outfitted in orange and black. "All right!" Ruhlman would cry through a bullhorn. "Whaddya say we given them a big Whompem-Stompem? One, two, three: Whomp-Em! Stomp-Em! Go Big O!" Years later, the Auditorium thunder would remind Lynne Lawson, then a sixth-grader on St. Paul's volleyball team, of the atmosphere Terry Pettit's Husker teams would create in time at Lincoln's NU Coliseum. Ogallala Auditorium "was the Coliseum before the Coliseum was the Coliseum," Lawson said.

Morgan's first state title team had another advantage. To help their daughters and their classmates hone their serve-receiving skills, Pastor Hornig and Lee Schroeder designed and built a homemade spiking machine that Morgan eagerly put to use. Hornig engineered the machine, which *Omaha World-Herald* sportswriter Steve Pivovar described after the 1975 season as a contraption made out of "irrigation tubing, bicycle parts, an electric motor, springs and some lumber." It shot a ball at a player every eight seconds. "It gave us an edge," said Schroeder, who made the *World-Herald*'s all-class All-State team that year.

Now in Class B, the Indians once more advanced to state in Scottsbluff. Morgan and his players stayed in private homes and ate their meals at his parents' nearby home in Mitchell. "He didn't want any distractions and wanted us all together," Schroeder said. "We traveled in station wagons. It was just this unbelievable faith in our ability to win."

Ogallala pounded Ord and then Wayne in straight sets to set up a final with 18-1 Waverly, winner of the state's first and only three Class B titles to that time. The high school shut down as hundreds of Ogallalans drove up U.S. Highway 26 to Scottsbluff's Cougar Palace. "That was the biggest group we'd ever played before," Morgan said. "There wasn't a place to sit anywhere."

Those who stayed home listened to Lungrin and his partner, the late Jim Thalken, on KIBC-FM (now KMCX). It was Nebraska's first play-by-play volleyball broadcast, said Lungrin, the Indians' volleyball "voice" through the 1983 season.

Before modern 25-point "rally scoring," high school matches were best-of-three with 15-point sets. Then and now, a team had to win a set by two, playing past 15 if need be. But teams could only score when serving. Waverly won the first set, 15–12, but Ogallala rallied to even the title match with a 15–6 second-set victory. At a critical point, with Ruhlman leading his town's fans in their Whompem-Stompem cheers, Morgan motioned to freshman Janet

Adkins, still another St. Paul's product, to come in and serve. "It was really intense, and she was just a freshman," Schroeder said. "This little freshman from St. Paul's comes in and serves like a machine. We had a huge run."

The Indians raced to a 7–0 third-set lead, but Waverly stormed back to lead 11–10. Ogallala recaptured the lead and, with the score 13–12, drove home the last two points. In what Pivovar called "perhaps the finest (match) ever played by Nebraska girls" up to that time, Morgan—and Ogallala—were state champions. "I remember the fans pouring onto the court," Schroeder said, "and I remember our male students trying to cut down the net and (us) having to tell them you can't do that in volleyball."

Morgan started his first summer volleyball camps in 1977, but he had a scheduling conflict. His wedding to Kate Mohr, who met Morgan while teaching at Progress–West Ward, fell on the camp's last day. Fortunately, he married a big volleyball fan. "In the early years, we watched the games at home on video," said Kate, who became her husband's statistician. "It really became kind of a family affair for us."

Diane Schroeder, who became a four-year scholarship starter for the Kansas Jayhawks, helped out at that first camp. That's where she first met "little Angie"—Angie Millikin, who was destined to help continue Ogallala's dynasty and build another. Millikin attended school in nearby Brule until sixth grade, when her mother transferred her to Ogallala. During her first lunch period in the Progress–West Ward gym, Morgan would get the girls to find a partner to practice "bumping," the initial hit after the ball comes over the net.

She hadn't yet played volleyball, Millikin said. And Tami Armstrong, her partner and eventual high school teammate, was way ahead of her. "I went to Brule for the weekend, and Kampfe's Store did not have a volleyball," she said. "But they had an orange plastic basketball that was the same size and virtually the same weight as a volleyball. So I used the roof as my partner and spent 10 hours a day that weekend, working long enough to be Tami Armstrong's partner."

Lynne Lawson joined the Indians in 1979, a year before Karen, as Morgan sought a sixth straight trip to state. They opened with a home victory over Sidney, then Ogallala's traditional first-weekend opponent. But neither the Lawson sisters nor their classmates would taste the state tournament—or beat the Red Raiders again—over four long years.

Coach Bill Willburn had been blessed with his own set of gifted young volleyball players—a group including Patty Hecht, Barbie Young and Linda Loeschen. "They could get under our skin like no other team," Lawson said. "Bill was a pain in my butt, and I was a pain in his," Morgan said. "It went that way for many years."

While Sidney was regularly beating Ogallala in the season's first and last matches, outstanding Minden teams twice snatched away the Southwest Conference title and won Class B in 1980. Ogallala finally recaptured the conference crown in 1981, but Sidney once more awaited as the Lawson sisters and Lynne's senior classmates Shelly McQuillan, Julie Moore and Dee Hoover rode the bus to the Class B-8 district final in Gering. For more than two hours, the Indians and Raiders slugged it out as a jam-packed gym roared after every sideout. But Sidney prevailed—15–13, 7–15, 15–11—en route to its first state title. "To me, it was the hardest-played game I'd ever played in my life," Lawson said.

History would repeat itself in 1982, after a district final even more memorable than the first. Angie Millikin had broken into Morgan's rotation, which also included such players as returning starter Lori Dealey and St. Paul's alumnae Karen Lawson, Jackie Morrow and Suzanne Reimann.

As yet another district final with Sidney approached, Millikin said, she wanted nothing more than to help the seniors slay the Raider dragon. The two titans met on the same Gering court to settle matters in a B-8 district so stocked with great teams, Lungrin says, that it deserved to be called the "mini state tournament." "It was in Gering, but it felt like an Ogallala game," Millikin said. "That's how well-attended it was. We had virtually the whole city there."

Typical five-set college matches, in this rally-scoring era, can run two hours. That night in November 1982, Sidney and Ogallala battled for two hours and 45 minutes. "We duked it out," Millikin said. "It was 1–1, 2–2, 3–3—nobody ever got a substantial lead." In the third set, "we really thought we had them—and then we didn't quite hang on."

The Raiders took it—15–17, 15–13, 15–10—en route to another Class B crown. But fate lent a hand in 1983. This time around, the Indians would play in the B-7 district, with most of their Southwest Conference partners but without Sidney. If the high-stakes rivalry were to continue, it would be on the state's biggest stage.

Loeschen had graduated, though Young remained to help guide Sidney toward a three-peat. But Millikin and her teammates finally stopped their nemesis in the season opener.

For the next two months, the top-ranked Indians and No. 2 Raiders steadily marched toward their inevitable destiny. It came in November's Class B final at Pershing Auditorium in Lincoln, where the state tournament had settled in 1981 after a four-year Kearney stopover. The 7,000-seat downtown arena sold out. "I remember they closed down Pershing," Morgan said. "It was chaos to get in."

The opening set was as closely matched as ever. The Indians fell behind 11–6 in the first set. Then they erupted with a rally into which they seemingly poured five years' worth of frustrations. "The sets I was hitting were in the perfect place," Millikin said. "I remember hitting the ball inside the 10-foot line and thinking, 'My gosh, we're on fire.'"

Morgan's Indians scored 24 of the match's last 29 points. They stormed back to take the first set, 15–11, then dominated the second set, 15–5. Morgan was back on top. "That's when I got to hold my firstborn (Ryan) up and see him crawl around the court and hold the trophy," he said.

Like Ogallala, Husker volleyball would enjoy early low-key success until its dynasty-maker came along. Pat Sullivan helped create a solid foundation before Pettit took over after the 1976 season. Like Morgan, he built on his predecessors' early victories but initially coached in front of tiny crowds. But the Huskers encountered quite a different scene on Sept. 22, 1979, when he brought his 11-0 Huskers to meet Northern Colorado halfway between the two schools—at the Ogallala Auditorium.

Pettit's team had walked into a volleyball madhouse. Two thousand Ogallala fans roared boisterously for the Huskers, who took Northern Colorado to the limit before losing in five sets. "We talked to the (Husker) girls after the match. They were awestruck," said Lungrin, who called the match on radio with Thalken. "I told them our high school girls played before crowds like that all the time."

Pettit said he doesn't remember much about the 1979 Ogallala match. But he said there's no doubt that the program Morgan built—especially his annual summer camps—played a significant role in developing volleyball throughout Nebraska. "Steve was one of several coaches I think was able to create an environment for volleyball to develop," he said. "It never happens by accident. It's because somebody is willing to go above and beyond in developing the sport . . . We never talked about this, but it helped he was an elementary P.E. teacher. He was able to develop the sport from both ends and make sure the kids were introduced to the fundamentals."

One of those kids, Morgan's own Angie Millikin, had committed to play for Nebraska before her final Ogallala state tournament game. She joined the team in 1985, and in 1986, Millikin's sophomore year, Nebraska advanced to its first NCAA championship match, in Stockton, California. Also part of that team was Sidney's Barbie Young, her one-time rival who became her lifelong close friend.

To get there, the Huskers trounced Stanford, one of several West Coast teams that had dominated the college game during those first post–Title IX years. "Stanford was especially vocal about us not deserving to be there," Millikin said. "And we creamed them."

The University of the Pacific beat the Huskers for the crown, but not before Millikin had indirectly introduced the nation to Ogallala. ESPN announcer Chris Marlow, she said, kept calling her over to press row to ask her how to spell and pronounce her hometown's name. Finally, she said, she stepped back and did a half-dozen jumping jacks while calling out the cadence Morgan had taught hundreds of his students: "O! G! A! L-L-A-L-A!" "And he said years later that's how he remembers it," Millikin said.

As the millennium turned, Steve Morgan would win his third and last state title—then watch another Angie he coached reach volleyball's national pinnacle. His Indian volleyball teams remained a formidable Class B force, posting second-place finishes in 1988, 1992, 1994 and 1995. Those last two runner-up teams were led by Angie Oxley, who like Millikin had shown her determination to master the game in Morgan's P.E. classes. "I remember his first competition was to get a hundred consecutive bumps," she said. "If you succeeded, you'd get this awesome little ribbon that said '100.' And then his next challenge was 200, 300, 400, all the way up to 1,000 . . . It took me to my fifth-grade year, but I did get to that 1,000."

As seventh-graders in 1992, Oxley and her volleyball-playing classmates were part of Ogallala's first offseason club volleyball team. They traveled to Kearney, Denver and especially Omaha for tournaments. Though Morgan organized the club squad, he asked Chappell High School coach Jim Behrends to coach it. Behrends' daughter, Kim, was Oxley's age and already showing promise as a future star. Bring her along, Morgan said.

Oxley and Kim Behrends played together on various clubs throughout high school. Pettit, who coached Nebraska's first national champion in 1995, was recruiting both of them. He offered Behrends a scholarship first—but she hesitated. Oxley didn't. But Behrends, who had several national scholarship offers, soon decided to join Oxley at Nebraska as a walk-on. She earned a scholarship a year later. Both joined the Huskers in 1997, a year after Pettit had recruited Wallace's Mandy Monson—one of the many players who had come from across the state to Morgan's summer camps.

The three Morgan-coached women played together on Pettit's final Husker squad in 1999. "We'd always see a Western Nebraska (sports) article with Kim and Mandy and I," Oxley said.

Oxley and Behrends returned as seniors when Cook, who had left a successful squad at Wisconsin to become Pettit's heir apparent, took over after coaching alongside him his last year. For his director of volleyball operations, Cook turned to another Ogallala veteran: Diane Schroeder Mendenhall, then head coach at Concordia University in Seward after holding the same position at York College.

Cook's first Husker team not only won the school's second national title but also posted a perfect 34-0 record. While Oxley took the floor for the NCAA final against Cook's former Wisconsin players, Diane Schroeder Mendenhall was thinking of Ogallala and Steve Morgan. And her parents, Pastor Hornig and St. Paul's. "Those thoughts are with me always," she said. "I was in Richmond, Virginia, after we won, looking around and saying, 'This is where we've come.'"

A month earlier, Morgan's Indians had once more reached the Class B championship at Pershing Auditorium. Led by such players as English Brodbeck, Erica Towell and Jayme Eichner—and including Morgan's own daughter Amanda—Ogallala won its third state title by upsetting top-ranked and undefeated Aurora, 15–13, 11–15, 15–10. "They were really hard workers," Kate Morgan said. "They were dedicated. They had that desire to win the state championship."

There would be many more state tournament visits, including an 11-year run from 2006 to 2016. All three Morgan children, including son Ryan, would play volleyball. His other daughter, Lindsay Nedlinski, helped coach the Indians by her father's side his last seven years. Neighboring Paxton, which boasts Keith County's other high school, has won six Class D state titles and long drawn on Morgan's expertise. He welcomed Cook's Huskers to Ogallala for exhibition spring volleyball matches in 2003 and 2016—before enthusiastic capacity crowds, of course.

He's watched from a distance as NU won three more national titles and introduced a nation to Nebraska volleyball madness as a then-NCAA record crowd of 17,209 jammed Omaha's CenturyLink Arena (now CHI Health Center Arena) to watch UNL capture the 2006 crown. Cook has promised Morgan courtside seats at the Bob Devaney

Sports Center, where its 8,000 seats are regularly sold out, any time he wants. "I can't tell you how many times I've heard the same story: 'He was my P.E. teacher,' 'I went to his camps,'" Cook said. "He has touched a lot of people in the state, and he's one of the reasons we call Nebraska Volleyball a state treasure."

And Morgan has seen many young women enjoy life-long success. Diane Schroeder Mendenhall would reach the upper echelon of UNL's administration, while older sister Pam Schroeder Borer taught and coached in Colorado. Lynne Lawson Werner became a nurse, a lawyer, a Grand Island bank president and leader of that city's airport authority. Angie Millikin tried her hand at volleyball coaching before becoming a sales manager for Newell Rubbermaid in Georgia and Arizona, where she now lives. And since 2002, a year after her NU playing career ended, Angie Oxley Behrens has sat on Creighton University's volleyball bench, helping build Coach Kirsten Bernthal Booth's Bluejays into an NCAA Sweet 16 and Elite Eight squad.

The coach who guided them all was inducted in 2012 into the Nebraska High School Hall of Fame. He retired as a P.E. teacher in 2013, but not until after the 2017 season did Morgan decide the next year would be his last as coach. "I didn't know what else I could do for the sport," he said. "I felt because of my age, it might be time for a younger person to take over." So Shelly Byrn, longtime coach at nearby St. Patrick High School in North Platte, took over the Indians in 2019. "She's no rookie," Morgan said. "She's been around the block, and she knows how to coach and work with kids."

After her hiring, Byrn told the *North Platte Telegraph*: "I have some very big shoes to fill." And some big dreams to inspire. That is what Morgan did for Millikin and hundreds of other young volleyball players. "He did a really good job of what I would call setting the dream and motivating you," she said. "It was about understanding what's out there, that there's a big 'ol world out there outside of Ogallala, Nebraska."

Oxley found it, in National Championship form. And thanks to Von Kampen, a St. Paul Lutheran product himself, the Ogallala volleyball story lives on. "The situation we have today in Nebraska, where volleyball and football each excite the entire state every fall, was exactly the way it was in Ogallala forty years ago. It wasn't just my hometown; it was the Lutheran church in Ogallala where I grew up where the seeds first sprouted and then spread to the whole town and then played its role in turning on the entire state."

Thanks to Morgan and the Schroeders and all the communities that had supporting parts, including one that got its name from a Texas town of some fame—a village that produced Doris Schroeder and one of the greatest Huskers of them all.

Fig. 1. The 1970–71 Huskers, who represented Nebraska at the National Intercollegiate Volleyball Championship in Lawrence, Kansas. *Top row, left to right*: Karen Ostrander, Elise Mahoney, Kathy Crewdson, Pam Rikli Miller, Jan Cheney, Peggy Tilgner. *Bottom row, left to right*: Linda Perry, Kathy Drewes, Coach Connie Ludwig, Dee Fentiman, Debbie Knerr. Ludwig was a graduate student at the time. (Nebraska Athletics)

**Fig. 2.** Husker star Jan Zink at the net during a 1974 match at Mabel Lee Hall. (Sandy Stewart)

**Fig. 3.** The 1974 Huskers having some fun at photo time. Coach Pat Sullivan's first team went 31-1 that season. (Sandy Stewart)

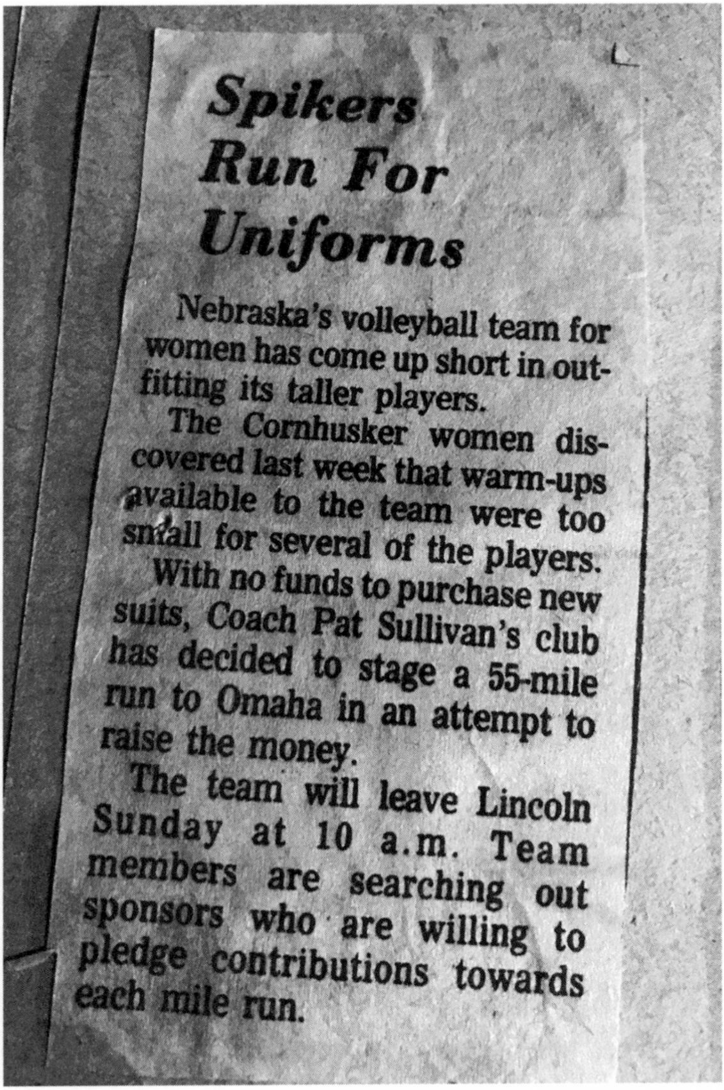

# Spikers Run For Uniforms

Nebraska's volleyball team for women has come up short in outfitting its taller players.

The Cornhusker women discovered last week that warm-ups available to the team were too small for several of the players.

With no funds to purchase new suits, Coach Pat Sullivan's club has decided to stage a 55-mile run to Omaha in an attempt to raise the money.

The team will leave Lincoln Sunday at 10 a.m. Team members are searching out sponsors who are willing to pledge contributions towards each mile run.

Fig. 4. The Lincoln and Omaha papers publicized the team's 1975 fundraiser, a run from Lincoln to Omaha to help the team raise money for uniforms. (Pat Sullivan)

**Fig. 5.** The 1975 Huskers, the first volleyball team officially recognized in the NU record books, with Coach Sullivan (*second row, far right*). (Nebraska Athletics)

Fig. 6. The 1980 media guide cover, with Terry Pettit in his fourth year as head coach. (Nebraska Athletics)

Fig. 7. Cathy Noth, pictured in a 1981 match at the Coliseum, was a star from the start—she just wasn't a setter from the start. (Nebraska Athletics)

Fig. 8. The 1981 Huskers finished 29-10 but were denied a spot in the first NCAA Tournament (Nebraska Athletics)

Fig. 9. (*opposite top*) Karen Dahlgren (*left*) and Lori Endicott (no. 2) teamed up for many big points for the Huskers in the 1980s. Both players had their jerseys retired in 2003. (Nebraska Athletics)

Fig. 10. (*opposite bottom*) Terry Pettit visiting with Athletic Director Bob Devaney and Husker assistant Jay Potter before a 1985 match at the Coliseum. (DeBoer family)

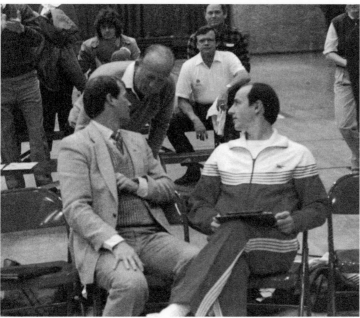

**Fig. 11.** Angie Millikin, Kathi DeBoer, and Barbie Young were teammates on some of the top Husker teams in the mid-1980s. (DeBoer family)

**Fig. 12.** The Huskers celebrating another Big Eight title in 1987. (Nebraska Athletics)

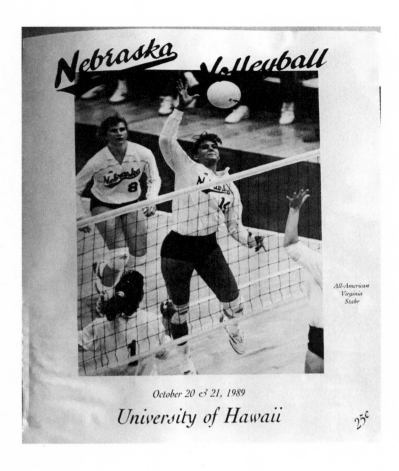

All-American
Virginia
Stahr

*October 20 & 21, 1989*

*University of Hawaii*

25¢

**Fig. 13.** From a family scrapbook: Virginia Stahr was on the cover of the program for the Nebraska-Hawaii matches in 1989. The Coliseum was packed to the rafters for both matches that weekend. (Stahr family)

**Fig. 14.** Husker Hall of Famer Janet Kruse was a three-time All-American and three-time Academic All-American. In 2021 she became the Huskers' team doctor. (Nebraska Athletics)

**Fig. 15.** The 1995 media guide cover, featuring captains Billie Winsett, Christy Johnson, and Allison Weston. (Nebraska Athletics)

**Fig. 16.** Kate Crnich was a regular starter as a junior and a star in helping NU win its first National Championship. (Nebraska Athletics)

**Fig. 17.** Fiona Nepo quickly became a fan favorite as a Husker. (Nebraska Athletics)

**Fig. 18.** The 1995 National Champions after their four-set victory over Texas in Amherst, Massachusetts. (Nebraska Athletics)

**Fig. 19.** (*opposite top*) Captains Christy Johnson, Allison Weston, and Billie Winsett with the National Championship trophy. (Nebraska Athletics)

**Fig. 20.** (*opposite bottom*) Karen Dahlgren, Tisha Delaney, and Enid Schonewise have remained close friends through the years. (Tisha Delaney Vandemore)

**Fig. 21.** (*opposite top*) Husker great Virginia Starr (Stahr)
(far right) was the assistant coach for the Big Horn Rams
team that won a Wyoming state title in 2021. (Alli Nikont)

**Fig. 22.** (*opposite bottom*) Former All-American Annie
Adamczak, next to her mural as part of Title IX anniversary
festivities in her home state of Minnesota. (Club 43)

**Fig. 23.** (*above*) Barbie Young, Lori Endicott, and Janet Kruse
at a Husker match in 2022. (Janet Kruse Sellon)

**Fig. 24.** (*opposite top*) Head Coach Christy
Johnson-Lynch and her Iowa State Cyclones
celebrating a win over No. 1 Texas, in 2022.
(Iowa State Athletics)

**Fig. 25.** (*opposite bottom*) Vicki Highstreet
(*left*) and Kathy Drewes with the Nebraska
Volleyball statue at the Devaney Center.
(John Mabry)

**Fig. 26.** (*above*) Pat Sullivan, Susie Heiser,
and Janice Kruger reunited at a Husker
match in 2022. (John Mabry)

**Fig. 27.** Pat Sullivan waves to the crowd as Jan Zink applauds during ceremonies to honor the 1974 and 1975 teams at the Devaney Center in 2022. (Nebraska Athletics)

# 10

## Waco

401. A number for the books. Greater than the population of Waco, Nebraska, by 150 or so, that .401 is also the career hitting percentage of Husker middle blocker Virginia Stahr. It's the best ever and has remained the record more than thirty years after Stahr's last match. The best in Nebraska Volleyball history and part of a story that comes with a slice of cherry pie that John Cook raves about to this day. That 401 is also not far off from the number of dollars in the Stahr family bank account most months when Virginia was growing up and just learning about life on the farm. Times were tough. Really tough. The farm crisis of the early 1980s hit the Stahrs hard. Peggy and Verle did their best to alleviate concerns at home. They did their best, period. "Mom told me she was applying for food stamps at one point. I didn't know that," said Virginia. "But I knew my dad was working so hard. He would farm during the day, and he'd be a machinist at night. He was just tired all the time."

By the way, the name is pronounced "stair" and not "star," although Virginia and her parents have mostly given up trying to correct strangers' mispronunciations. Virginia actually changed her name to Virginia Starr as part of a personal transformation project in Big Horn, Wyoming. We will get to that, but first, there was Waco. Born in 1877 when the railroad came through York County for the first time, the village was named after Waco, Texas, because one of the community's key founders had grown up there.

The Stahr place has been around since 1888. Verle has lived there since 1947. He and Peggy got married in 1957. "Verle farmed the land from before we were married until he retired in 2000," Peggy said. "In the early years he and his dad worked together raising alfalfa, wheat, and corn. They built up a dairy herd to allow the farm to support two families. Verle milked around a hundred cows at the peak and this continued until the farm crisis when we had to sell the cows—and stood in danger of losing the land to the bank."

Peggy said at one point they wouldn't have made it if neighbors hadn't been kind enough to provide hay for their cows. They also had the gift of a program that made it possible for them to house and hire workers from Japan to assist with the farm. "Thankfully," she said, "we were able to make it through those difficult years, which were also Virginia's volleyball career years."

The five Stahr kids went to Centennial High in nearby Utica. Like many of her classmates, Virginia played a lot of different sports for the Broncos. Basketball. Volleyball. Track and field. And she helped with the chores at home. "I always wanted to be outside." Mostly, anyway. "Cutting hay . . . I never, ever want to do that again." But there were benefits. "I got paid. I got a suntan." She also played softball as part of a town team. "I was lucky to be in a class with a lot of good athletes, so we had a really good team. We were playing softball with teams from Lincoln and Omaha at state. We were that good despite only having about two hundred people."

But softball was not her favorite. Neither was volleyball. "Basketball was my sport. I loved basketball. I felt volleyball was just something you did to get ready for basketball." It was Centennial's volleyball coach, Phyllis Rice, who got Virginia ready for greatness. Rice led Stahr and the Broncos to their first state championship in 1984. "Coach Rice, she really started it for me," Stahr said. "She made the game bigger for me. It was about spirituality. It was about who you were as a person. She was just there. Solid. Caring. I don't know if I would have made it at Nebraska without her helping me. She helped me believe in myself early on. We won the town's first state championship. It was pretty special. We were a bunch of girls who were full of ourselves, but she could bring us together. I owe a lot to her."

Through volleyball Virginia earned and made the most of that scholarship her family needed so badly. "That is something I wasn't aware of, the value of a college scholarship," she said, "until I started sending my own kids to school."

Stahr went to a Husker team volleyball camp while she was at Centennial, and she was impressive enough that Terry Pettit asked her to come back for an individual camp for the top players. "At that time, it cost $150. I said, 'I don't have $150.' So I went home and Mom and Dad and I sat down, and we decided I would pay $75 and they would pay $75." It resulted in a scholarship. "So I figured that was the best $75 investment I ever made in my life."

Her mom said that at first the courtship with the Huskers was a lot to handle. "Although Virginia had excelled in high school, we were a bit overwhelmed when Jay Potter came to our home on a recruiting visit," Peggy said. "Jay even told Virginia that if she worked hard she would likely become an All-American. Wow!"

The Stahrs thought the All-American talk was crazy. Not possible. "But it was an attractive thought," Peggy said.

Virginia joined the Husker program, and so did Peggy. She was appointed as secretary of the new volleyball booster club at NU, the Match Club. "We had many meetings, and I helped with the club newsletter," Peggy said.

The Match Club was the brain child of Pettit, and it began in Lincoln at the home of Kari and Tom Beckenhauer. "Always a visionary, Terry Pettit asked a few folks to gather one evening in 1985 to form a booster club for Husker volleyball," Kari said. "After discussion of what he was looking for, a board was formed, and things commenced."

Vicki Ossenkop (Highstreet) was the first president. Kathy Drewes and Nancy Grant (Colson) and Tom Beckenhauer were all part of the Match Club start-up. Peggy Stahr was the communications specialist for the new group. "Tom Beckenhauer gathered the information and sent it to me. I formatted it and sent it back to him for printing and dissemination."

Meanwhile, Virginia was becoming a headliner in Lincoln, but it didn't happen without plenty of nervous moments. "I went in pretty scared," she said. "I wasn't a very good volleyball player when I started. My skill set was really behind. I was super-scared going in. I didn't feel like I belonged." She spent one season learning the ropes as a redshirt, which meant she could spend a year developing her skills without losing a year of eligibility. For the first month of practice she was on a different Coliseum court, working on defense and passing basics. "I get why they did it, but talk about being humbled. I think I learned resilience, hard work, and having faith despite the circumstance, because it didn't feel real good at first."

But from time to time she would remember how Jay Potter thought she was All-American caliber. That stayed with her. "That was pretty significant, to hear that, and not believe it but still tuck it away somewhere and keep striving." And she had teammates who wanted to see her succeed, starting with Karen Dahlgren, of course. "She was kind of my mentor. She was very similar to me, a small-town athlete. I really respected her a lot. I still do."

And Coach Rice was there for her too. "Even when I was

in college, she came to every one of my games. Seeing her in the stands helped me, when things were hard and I was scared." In time Virginia, at "barely six feet," was killing it, with power and accuracy. The ball was hitting the floor with force, time after time. A move from outside to middle paid big dividends. "I feel like I have some weird ability to see things. Some vision, that I could see the holes. I don't know what that was about. Some weird intuitive thing," she said. "And it's because I had really good setters. I had Lori Endicott my junior year. She was just this phenomenal setter. I had Val Novak [as a senior], and she was good, too. I had really good setters."

Ask those who were there, and the word "fierce" comes up time and time again. "Virginia was a fierce competitor," Endicott said. "She brought a high level of intensity and fire every time she stepped on the court. Competitiveness, along with athleticism, made her a force as a middle blocker." A young assistant at the time would say the same. "In my early days of coaching," Cook said, "she was one of the most fierce competitors I've ever seen."

Virginia said the coaches helped bring out the fierce in her. Although Stahr and Pettit had their tense player-coach moments, the player knew the coach always had a reason for the buttons he pushed. "The good things outshine the bad things. I don't think you can have an athlete excel without pushing them. Pettit knew how to get the best out of me. I am not an angry person, but on the court he would get that part of my nervous system going."

Virginia made her mark with a strong freshman season in 1986 when the Huskers went to their first Final Four. She made the All-Big Eight second team with an impressive .367 hitting percentage, which is a way of measuring attacking success. It is calculated by taking a player's kills and subtracting hitting errors and dividing the total by number of attacks (or swings). As a sophomore she led the Big Eight by hitting .397, so close to that elusive .400, which is a big deal in volleyball just like it's a big deal in baseball. Not many ever get there for a career. In 1987 Stahr also contributed in a big way with 129 block assists and a team-leading 63 service aces.

After that All-Big Eight season she had one of the greatest seasons in Husker history as a junior, hitting .404. Virginia had 11 matches with a percentage of .500 or better and had an incredible 31 kills in a match against Texas, the 1988 National Champs. But there was a painful price. That .400-hitting right shoulder was hurting. "My shoulder really began to trouble me midseason my junior year. It started with the lingering ache and then kept escalating to where the pain was constant. Back in those days we took a lot of anti-inflammatory meds and lived on ice. Unfortunately, it then began to sub lux whenever I reached outside my body in an extended position, especially digging balls and reaching for sets."

Doctors weighed in with various opinions. Virginia recalls a two-hour wait in one Lincoln medical office, which would likely never happen in 2022 for a Husker volleyball star, but it happened in January of 1989. "My diagnosis was a hyper mobile joint that would sub lux when stressed. Instability of the labrum and surrounding tissue. I could have one surgery, which had more chance of success but would limit my range of motion to just 90 degrees, pretty much eliminating any chance of an arm swing, or I could get the surgery with 30 percent chance of full recovery, but I would have full ROM. I opted for the second option."

She thanks Dr. Tom Heiser, brother of former Husker Susie Heiser, for some top-flight surgical work and the chance to finish her Nebraska career on a high note. Virginia's senior season had it all. The highs and the lows and everything in between. But also thanks to adjustments on her part, there was no dropoff in performance or value to the team. "She was a great competitor and she had an amazing transformation when she couldn't swing like she used to after the shoulder surgery," Cook said. "She still found a way with her intelligence and her volleyball IQ."

And the 1989 Huskers, with Stahr and Carla Baker as the only seniors, found their way to the Final Four for the second time in program history. NU started the season 14-0 and won their fourteenth straight Big Eight title, going 12-0 in league play. No. 14 Stahr helped lead the way, along with sophomore star Janet Kruse and Novak, a junior setter from the Chicago area. All three received All-America honors.

The Huskers knocked off Minnesota and Illinois in the Lincoln regional, which meant another trip to the National Semifinals, this time in Hawaii. But the host school, ranked No. 1 in the nation, had been eliminated by Long Beach State, so the Huskers became fan favorites in Honolulu. The weekend got off to a great start with a sweep of mighty UCLA, which replaced Hawaii as the top-ranked team.

Against the Bruins, four NU players had double digits for kills: Cris Hall with 19, Kruse with 12, Eileen Shannon with 11, and Stahr with 10. But the championship against Long Beach and their superstar, Tara Cross, was just the opposite. NU got smoked in three, 15–12, 15–0, 15–6. Yep, 15-zip in the second set. Cross had 20 kills and hit .529. Not another day in paradise for the red team. Pettit said it was Cross and Long Beach State's speed that got the better of the Huskers. He also said that he and Cook spent a couple of days on a hotel rooftop in Honolulu trying to figure out what hit them. No joke.

Novak, another standout in the long line of Husker All-Americans at the setter position, said it wasn't funny at the time, not at all, but she said it's easier to smile about it these many years later. "You have to understand ,we do hold the record that will never be broken, being beaten fifteen-zero in a National Championship match," she said. "We all laugh about it. I can't take away anything from Long Beach State. They were a phenomenal team. That team, wow, they were just unbelievable athletes and we just weren't ready for them.

"You can't take away from the fact that we battled to get there. I don't even know if we were supposed to be there. We battled to get there and then we won the first match."

The loss to Long Beach was difficult for some. It was crushing for Virginia Stahr. "After we lost the championship, it was pretty rough. I'm not going to lie. It was a hard day. I'm so competitive. That really broke my spirit a little bit, which I'm not proud to say. I wish I could have been stronger. So I was ready to walk away for a little while. In time it's come back. John has been so great about bringing us back as alumni in celebration of that season."

It was a season to celebrate, and Virginia had a Husker career to celebrate. With her injury she didn't have as many attacks as a senior, but she made each one count. Her .440 hitting percentage for the year—no. 3 all-time at Nebraska through 2021—put her at .401 lifetime, a school record that has yet to be topped. "To do that," Cook said, "first of all you have to have a great arm. But that was taken away a little bit with the surgery. Second of all, you have to have great vision. What the really good middles do, they have great vision."

She also finished with 159 career aces (number three all-time) and 555 blocks (number six). She was the Big Eight Female Athlete of the Year in 1989. She won just about every award in the book that season, and not just the athletic kind. She excelled in the classroom while working on her elementary education degree. "She was very inspiring," Kruse said, "and someone I looked up to academically."

Stahr was an Academic All-American and received the prestigious Delta Scholar Athlete of the Year Award and the NCAA Today's Top Six Award, which recognized the nation's best at combining athletic and academic excellence. Now the Top 10 Award, it is one of the NCAA's highest honors.

Another thing that took some of the sting away was a family trip to Japan after the Final Four. The Stahrs' finances had improved somewhat, and they had saved to make it possible to travel for the Final Four and beyond, to visit some old friends who had helped them when times were tough. "Virginia was so devastated after the game, she just didn't want to go with us," Peggy said. "We had tickets to Japan from Hawaii. Virginia begged to stay behind, but we thought it better for her to have a change of venue as planned, rather than staying behind to grieve alone. We spent several weeks in Japan visiting the young Japanese men who had worked on our dairy farm with us and lived in our home. It was so exciting to meet them again and their families."

Through all of it Peggy said they tried to make sure folks realized there were five kids in the family, not just one. "They all have interesting stories. We tried really hard to balance that, too, because she was getting a lot of notoriety."

Virginia's story includes a master's degree (curriculum and instruction), a teaching stint at Boys Town, physical-therapy school, a marriage and a divorce, and four daughters. She beams when she talks about that part of the story. Her girls. Their journey took them to Utah and Wyoming, most recently the town of Big Horn, where she is a spiritual healer who, according to her website, "specializes in working with the nervous system of anyone struggling with headache, pain, depression, and anxiety. In balancing the nervous system, true healing occurs which results in the possibility of living a life full of vitality and purpose."

She also goes by the name of Virginia Starr now—not Stahr and not Gee, her married name. With the blessing of her family and her daughters, she is Virginia Starr. "I didn't want to be a Gee, or a Stahr. That's who I was . . . felt like such a failure after divorce. Star means transformation, and people say it Star anyway." A friend said it was the perfect name for what she does. "It's not that I'm running away. I'm transforming. I didn't want to go back."

Not that she doesn't like to talk about those Waco days and her family. Not at all. She was the fourth child. Fifth was David, who was hired as the volleyball coach at McCool Junction, Nebraska, in 2020. "I love it," Virginia said, "because I felt bad. He hated being dragged to all my games. And the poor guy, wherever he went, it was 'Oh, you're Virginia's brother.' That gets old when you're young."

Big Sis also found her way into coaching. Alli Nikont is glad she did, too. Nikont was hired as the head volleyball coach at Big Horn High in 2020. She was new to the area (just south of the Montana border) and needed an assistant. The athletic director mentioned that one of the seniors had a mom who played at Nebraska.

"I didn't believe him," Nikont said. "I was like *the Nebraska*?"

"Well, then Virginia did apply, and I kind of felt like I was being punked, reading her resume. It was pretty impressive. Just to have that kind of resource in our community, I was pretty excited about it. We interviewed her and I hired her right away. So we started this thing together last year [in 2020]."

In 2021 they took "that thing" all the way to the top. The Big Horn Rams were Class 2A Champs for the first time in twelve years. Nikont said Virginia played a major role while rarely sharing anything about her Nebraska days. "I love to pick her brain. She is so humble. It is hard to get her to talk about things. You don't really know until you know, so I started to google her after I hired her, and the more you read, it's just so impressive. It was just jaw-dropping to know that she was in our gym, and the girls have watched those videos. She's been an awesome assistant. The way she reads the court and sees plays develop before they happen is pretty awesome."

That vision made her one of the best in Husker history. "In Wyoming, we have plenty of long bus rides," Nikont said. "I have picked her brain. I want to know all the things. She's done things that we can only dream about, her experiences."

The experiences of a Nebraska High School Hall of Famer who did remarkable things as a Husker. "She was extraordinary," Pettit said. With some pretty special memories.

They are welcome again, those memories. "My favorite memory, during Regionals, it was Christmas and they'd play 'Jingle Bells,' and the crowd would all take out their keys and jingle them. It was very cool. But the coolest part was when you were walking up from that dungeon, our locker room down in the basement of the Coliseum, we'd be walking up the steps and we could hear the band playing and the crowd. That was pretty exciting. And now, when I walk into Devaney, it just blows me away."

The Stahr cherry tree is gone, along with the world famous pie that a young Husker assistant coach loved so much. "That is embedded in John's mind," Peggy said. "For a Match Club gathering I took a cherry pie for the group meal and one for John. He teases me about it still. Unfortunately, the cherry tree blew over, so I'm not making cherry pies anymore." The tree might be gone, but when Peggy and Verle think back, they still marvel at all of it. "It's interesting to see that Virginia still holds some of the records in NU volleyball history," Peggy said. "Who would have thought such a thing could happen?"

It's usually not difficult to find any of their seventeen grandchildren on the field or court. They are usually wearing no. 14, in honor of Aunt Virginia. One of the greats. And of all the great attackers in Husker history, there's only one career .400 hitter in the bunch. There's only one Virginia.

The way her Husker career ended in 1989 does not hurt as

much now. She feels the value and meaning of it now that a few years have passed. She also recognizes what it meant to her parents. It meant a lot. "I didn't understand when I was playing how much it meant to them. That's what came back and gives me so much joy, to know that they got so much joy out of something I was doing."

With time she has also been able to mend fences with Pettit. They didn't part on friendly terms in 1989. They are friends now. "I have so much respect for him now," she said, "plus I was a cocky pain in the ass, so I might have deserved some of it."

She is grateful for the eye-opening lessons she took from Pettit and Cook during her five years in the Husker program. "They opened up that world to me, being able to see beyond what's in front of you. They're both so good at that. You're talking about a play and then you're talking about the world, how this play parallels this world situation. They just do that naturally. I appreciated that, them making my world bigger, through volleyball." And it doesn't getting any bigger than .401.

# 11

# Blair

College recruiting had its challenges before smartphones and Google Maps. In the fall of 1987 Terry Pettit had received directions to the home of a top prospect who lived in an off-the-beaten-path area about ninety minutes from Lincoln. The coach was struggling to locate the home between Blair and Fort Calhoun while learning that the path was actually starting to turn rough. He stopped to ask another resident in the area for a little help. To paraphrase, that neighbor said 'You just go up the road a bit and the next left-hand turn is the driveway. And oh, by the way, the Oklahoma coach was just there the other day, and the same for the Iowa coach and a bunch of others.

Yes, Janet Kruse (Sellon) was a prospect of some talent, and not just because of her athletic skills. She was one sharp cookie, too. "She had great size, great hands," Pettit said. "And she had great intention in everything she did. She was very bright."

Bright enough to know, as she entered her teens, that she was outgrowing some of her childhood activities in Blair, 30 miles north of Omaha and just across the Missouri River from Iowa. "It was a Class B school," Kruse said, "so you got to do a little bit of everything. My brother was pretty athletic, so my mom threw me in with whatever he was doing,

111

so we actually got started young doing some swimming and things like that. Probably in junior high was when I got serious about sports. We showed horses. We did 4-H. So that was big in my life when I was younger."

She was involved in Pony of the Americas, a special breed, but there was one problem with the ponies when Janet got to junior high. Little horsies and tall kiddos don't always make for the perfect match. "My legs started kind of dragging on the ground," said Kruse, who was 6 feet 1 when she became a Husker, "so I thought it was probably time to switch and went on to do some other things. I did show choir. I did dance. I did band."

She was grateful for the variety in her life and for life on the farm. "My grandpa farmed. We had cattle. We raised a lot of our own crops. I am very appreciative of that background." She also appreciated the chance to play volleyball with her younger sister, Jodi. "Some of the memories I have that I really cherish are playing with her because she was a setter, so it was really ideal having your sister being the setter so you can kind of tell her where to set you and adjust. There is definitely a bond there and level of communication that I think is unique for sisters, and being able to play with her was really fun. She ultimately ended up going to Georgia to play for them."

Janet was a Husker from 1988 to 1991. She got noticed at a Nebraska camp the summer after her sophomore year at Blair. "Enid Schonewise was my camp coach. I remember her talking to Coach Pettit about me being there and talking about my athleticism. I was not a fine-tuned volleyball player." Watching Schonewise and Karen Dahlgren and Tisha Delaney leading the camp was a motivating force. "Watching them doing demonstrations, I really thought 'Man, if I could do that, that would be awesome.'"

Janet was also recruited for basketball by Midland Lutheran

in nearby Fremont and other area schools. Rice was interested in her as a high jumper. For volleyball it came down to Big Eight rivals Nebraska and Oklahoma. Her Husker host was Becky Bolli, and it was a pretty easy decision after that visit to Lincoln. "I loved the players and being close to home, so family could watch."

The Huskers also had a new assistant when Kruse entered the program, and that newcomer knew right away that Kruse was not just another recruit. "She was a tremendous, dynamic hitter," John Cook said, "and we were just trying to decide whether to put her on the left or the right. She ended up playing on the right for us. Just a powerful, dynamic attacker. Obviously very smart. Early in my coaching career I recall conversations with athletes about what they wanted to do with their major and what they wanted do with their life. You start having those conversations. But when you are a kid out of high school, it's just about how do you get through the day."

Not the case with Kruse. She had big plans and big dreams. Cook remembers those conversations well. "She always said 'I'm gonna be a doctor.' I would kid her and say 'Okay, great, when I get old you'll take care of me.' She said 'Sure, yeah.'" Yes, Janet Kruse wanted to be a doctor. She just wanted to play some more volleyball first. And did she ever. Kruse would become the program's first three-time All-American, with first-team honors in 1989 and 1990 and second-team recognition in 1991, a season that was hampered from the start because of an ankle injury.

She said star setter Val Novak (Warrior) had a lot to do with her success. Novak, another hitter-turned-setter, was a two-time All-American from the Chicago suburb of Oak Lawn, Illinois. She was the Big Eight Player of the Year as a senior in 1990 and remains near the top of the Husker career charts in assists and aces (second behind Jordan Larson's 161). Her 13.74 assists per set in 1989 was tops in the nation, and the Huskers never finished with a ranking worse than fifth in her four seasons, including two Final Four appearances. "Such an incredible leader," Kruse said. "Great to play with. Because I was a right-side, we trained quite a bit together. Val just always had a way to keep you confident and make you smile. She was a fierce competitor and great leader at the same time." And a great friend to the world. "My grandpa adored Val," Kruse said, "because she was the first one to come over and give you a hug."

Kruse said she was surrounded by a cast of inspiring Huskers. One of them was Cris Hall. "We were very different, but we were best of friends playing. I was more laid back, a little timid. Cris was very intense, kind of more in-your-face, but we got along great and balanced each other out well. She was also really inspiring because she worked really, really hard. She was actually a track athlete coming in with raw talent and hadn't had as much volleyball experience coming in as some of the rest of us."

Another teammate, Stephanie Thater, was an All-American herself. "Steph was a huge player for us in the middle," Kruse said. "A lot of memories with her and Eileen Shannon as an outside hitter. Of course, Linda Barsness. Becky Bolli was our jump server, and back then they didn't have a libero, so she would come in and rip off some top-spin serves that were pretty hard to pass for a lot of people because that wasn't as common as it is now."

Pettit said Kruse was a pro at passing and all aspects of the game. "Janet was probably as good a primary passer, or certainly one of the top passers, that we've ever had," he said. "She was also a tremendous blocker and tremendous attacker. She was a six-rotation player and was really exceptional. I remember sitting on the bench, and Debbie Brand was sitting next to me. Debbie, at that point, was a back-row sub. And I said to her, 'How do we win? What do we do to win?' Debbie gave me the right answer: basically we keep the ball in play until we get it in system and then set Janet. She was the terminator.

"During that span we were very successful against Texas, and some of that was the defense that Texas ran because she had the ability to go over the right side and their block and put the ball between the line and the middle defender. They didn't adjust to that, and I can remember that being the key factor in having success against Texas at that time." The Huskers won six out of seven sets against the Longhorns in winning the 1990 and 1991 matches between the two programs.

Kruse and Company made it back to the National Semifinals in 1990, but it was another loss to Pacific—this time 3–1—that ended their season. That one went 15–13, 11–15, 15–9, 15–12. Hall led NU with 18 kills. Novak had 46 assists and 17 digs. The Huskers won 16 straight matches in getting to the Final Four, including sweeps over Pitt and Penn State in the Regionals in Lincoln, and the team's 32-3 record was the best in program history at the time.

The Coliseum was home to 3,031 fans per night in 1990, the best attendance in the nation, but it was time for some home improvement, with updates to make the facility more volleyball-friendly. "We played my senior season in Devaney," Kruse said, "because they were renovating the Coliseum, and just going into that big, open arena was a change because you didn't have the fans right on top of you. Now I look back on that and there's a lot of history there that some of the current players probably don't have any idea about, how different things were. I remember going to Missouri, and there might be 100 people there."

The Huskers started the 1991 season 7-0, but that start also included a sprained ankle for Kruse during the season-opening tournament at Kentucky. She said it bothered her most of the year and led to a lot of time on a stationary bike during practices.

Pettit said injuries and ailments were a big issue that season, right to the end. The Huskers, playing NCAA tournament matches at the Devaney Center while renovation work was happening at the Coliseum, beat Illinois and Wisconsin in three sets before falling to Ohio State in a four-set Regional final—15–9, 9–15, 16–17, 7–15. "Eileen Shannon couldn't play because she was sick," Pettit said. "[Our] team was a Final Four team, or had the talent to certainly be there. Ohio State played extremely well. They played well in the final four. If you're playing the right schools, playing the best schools, you're always going to have that possibility. All you can do is keep putting yourself in position."

All the while, Kruse was putting herself in position to be a success after college. "I knew there'd be life beyond volleyball. I just didn't quite know what that was." Kruse was honored as Academic All-American of the Year in each of her final two seasons at Nebraska and capped it with an NCAA Today Top Eight Award. There was no greater honor for a student-athlete. After her Husker playing days, Kruse considered playing professionally in Europe. "It was not as lucrative at the time," she said. "Medical school won out."

Maybe you heard. Janet Kruse, Nebraska's first three-time All-American, wanted to be a doctor. And that is what she became, getting her medical degree from the University of Nebraska Medical Center and joining Lincoln Family Wellness in 1999. Kruse, who is also one heck of a pianist, gave a lot of thought to becoming a pediatrician because of how much she loved kids, but she chose family practice so she could help more people.

In 2004, her No. 17 jersey was retired by the Huskers, and in 2016 she was inducted into the University of Nebraska Athletic Hall of Fame. Good thing Pettit found the Kruse place, as it turned out. A really good thing. "I just feel honored that I got to play for him," she said.

Cook feels that too, and their work together was not complete. On November 3, 2021, Coach Cook Tweeted the news that the Huskers had a new team doctor. The team's first female doctor. Guess who? Dr. Janet Kruse Sellon.

> Today was her first day as our team doctor for female student-athletes. Epic day for Nebraska Athletics.

All part of an epic Husker story. Novak knows it well. "I trusted she would get the job done during crunch time," Val said, "and she delivered consistently." Yes she did. And did you know this? Kruse, the All-American MD, is believed to be the only Husker to have delivered more than a thousand kills and more than a thousand babies. Epic.

# 12

# Heights and Sounds

John Cook, who talks often about the importance of "the journey," was a club volleyball coach in San Diego, his hometown, when Terry Pettit asked him about making Nebraska part of the Cook journey in the summer of 1988. The two did not know each other well, but they had become acquainted through mutual friends and volleyball events in San Diego. Pettit wanted Cook to join the Husker staff as an assistant coach. There's a story here, and it includes Ogallala. It had to. In his book *Dream Like a Champion*, Cook shared:

> Nebraska flew me out for an interview. It was maybe my second or third time on a plane. I got to Lincoln and they put me up at the Cornhusker Hotel, an opulent landmark in the heart of downtown. For a teacher and coach whose vacations consisted of taking his wife hiking and then sleeping in the truck, showing up to a fancy hotel and having a gift bag waiting felt like the big time.
>
> I did not have to think too hard about taking that job either. Next stop: Nebraska.
>
> We pulled into Ogallala on August 5, 1988. We had been towing a rented trailer full of all our belongings behind our Toyota pickup truck for 1,300 miles. It was a 105-degree day and the nearby feedlot smelled like feed-

lots tend to smell in 105-degree heat. We got to our motel room, opened the door, flipped on the light, and watched as cockroaches scattered.

This was Wendy's introduction to our new home state. She started sobbing. "Where are you taking me?" she asked. "If this is Nebraska, we're out of here."

"No. Lincoln is a little different," I said.

And it was different. For me it was a little bit of a dream destination. Not only was I joining a volleyball program that was serving notice that the sport could flourish at the college level outside of California, but I was also going to have the opportunity to study Nebraska's powerful football program up close.

Ogallala, with its love of volleyball, eventually won John over in a big way, and Nebraska Football, with the program's grand history—and its five National Championships (two at that time)—played a role in Cook's decision to come to Lincoln. Five national titles. Wouldn't it be something if the Nebraska Volleyball program could do that some day?

Pettit saw Nebraska Football as a vital partner, and not just because Memorial Stadium made a good place to advertise. It was a short walk from the Coliseum, and that's where he and an assistant would post flyers to promote upcoming volleyball matches, with the offer of free or $1 admission with a football ticket. "It would take us three hours because there were restrooms everywhere," he said. "We embraced football. I think some schools made a mistake and tried to separate themselves. I think we were influenced by Nebraska Football. On the recruiting trail, if we were out recruiting someone outside the state, the family might not be familiar with Nebraska Volleyball but they were familiar with football. I half-jokingly would say, but it was accurate, that if you want to build a program that can win a National Championship, and you're a volleyball coach, you either need to be able to look out the window at the ocean or have an I-back that runs for 1,500 yards. Either one of those was an entrée into the recruiting process."

Adding Cook to the program in 1988, after Jay Potter moved on to a coaching position in Illinois, didn't seem like a big deal to outsiders at the time, but it became a really big deal. And in 1990, with two Final Four appearances behind them, the Huskers entered a new decade on a roll, with lots of fans joining the party, too. Learning along the way.

Ed and Sue Tricker of Lincoln were among those who became fans at that time. They have been hooked ever since. Sue remembered one match back then when she and Ed started to leave with the Huskers up two games to one. "We didn't realize you had to win three," she said. "One of the things I remember early on," Ed said, "was one of the Nebraska players was Becky Bolli from Burwell, and she had the first jump serve I had ever seen, and that was like 'Wow.'"

And some of the "wow" crowds at the Coliseum were starting to draw the attention of the fire marshal. Like a 1989 weekend doubleheader with Hawaii. Oh, did folks come out for that. Janet Kruse (Sellon) remembers it well. "My junior year, when Hawaii came to play, that was the best environment to have," she said, "with fans kind of hanging over the court and loud. Those were some pretty incredible matches." Many fans had to turn back and head for home. Packed houses both nights. Dr. Hibner would throw up her hands, mostly with a smile, and say, "Guess we just have to pay the fire marshal's fine."

Crowds got bigger and bigger as Kruse and her name helped make a name for Husker PA announcer Steve Johnsen, who became a fan favorite. Johnsen's famous "Kruuuuuuse" call still rings in the minds of many fans, although initially Janet said she had to explain to family and friends that she was not being booed.

Steve and his wife and Vicki, the spotter during matches, became fan favorites for many years, and were asked to do the announcing and spotting for many NCAA Final Fours. "Steve and Vicki were very good at it," Janet said. "They're quite a duo. We were really, really fortunate to have those guys."

And University of Nebraska female athletes were oh so fortunate to have Dr. Hibner.

Kari Beckenhauer said she and her husband, Tom, would occasionally dine with Barb and would discuss Husker Athletics and Bob Devaney's desire to hire the best coaches for all sports, not just the men. "Terry Pettit has called Dr. Hibner 'our angel,' and he meant it," Kari said. "Dr. Hibner often pulled all-nighters, as if she were still a college student and set the groundwork for all women's sports at Nebraska. She grew up in Pennsylvania and went to school in Pennsylvania, New York, and Texas before coming to UNL with her PhD in hand. At her funeral in 2007—she died of cancer at age sixty-five—it was noted that SOB didn't mean Sweet Ol' Barb. Nope. She was driven to help women succeed on the big stage."

Hibner and Pettit gained a new ally when Bill Byrne was hired as athletic director in 1992. Bob Devaney retired (moving to an emeritus role), opening the door for Byrne to come to Lincoln after a successful run at the University of Oregon.

Meanwhile, additional progress came in the form of much-needed facility improvements at the Coliseum, which had become part aviary. "That was when air conditioning was added," Beckenhauer said. "That was a big deal, as the building only had a few tiny windows on the east and west sides that people would open. Birds flying in but not finding their way out was a problem, too. But you usually had to open the front doors to get some air flow during the warmer months.

New scoreboards were added, and times were a-changing, except on the big Longines clock on the south brick wall. It took a few more years before that was telling the proper time.

"One night, when the Coliseum was full, a bat had flown in and attached itself on the south (brick) wall—not as high as the Longines clock, but somewhat above the crowd. The crowd was terrified until one fan took off his heavy-heeled shoe and killed it. It was a relief for everyone, save for the bat.

"As crowds increased over time, folks would often drop off their kids at the door and then return after the match to pick them up. The problem was, there was no pay phone in the Coliseum, and this was before mobile phones. The Match Club asked Lincoln Telephone & Telegraph to install a pay phone, and they did because it was a moneymaker for them. This I knew because I was working at LT&T at the time."

More credit to Dr. Hibner, a common theme. "She was out and about to be seen and to promote her product, which was Husker women's sports," Beckenhauer said. "You'd see her at sporting events, but only at a distance, because she never promoted herself. If she saw you coming to do an interview with her about herself or her work, out the back door she went. Behind the scenes she helped many an athlete—both men and women—who needed work-study to survive financially during their time at UNL. One remodel of the Coliseum was to the second floor, south side. This resulted in offices for softball, volleyball, and Dr. Hibner, along with a much-needed conference room, which is where the softball and volleyball booster clubs would meet. She was in the middle of everything on purpose—she was going to make things work."

A lot of it worked thanks to the Match Club, with the Beckenhauers and several others paving the way. It was a key moment when John Cripe joined in 1987. Like Kari, he can share some great stories from those early days. John credits his wife, Judy, for getting him involved through her work at what is now US Bank. "I had never seen a collegiate volleyball match," Cripe said. "I had never been to a Nebraska game. Around that time Terry Pettit said he was looking for someone to manage the booster club. I said I had never seen a game and that's probably not a good idea."

But Cripe eventually agreed, and as it turned out he was president for twenty years. "I think we had $800 in the bank, and we ordered $2,000 worth of T-shirts for the first weekend. We didn't have the money to cover it. Sold them all within two games and kept adding to it. So, financially, that became part of our business structure. Ultimately, around the time I left I think we were selling $100,000 worth of T-shirts each year. Then the university took over in the mid-2000s because they could see we were making a profit."

One of Bill Byrne's first to-do items in 1992 was to develop a strong reserved-season-ticket program for volleyball. "I had a chance to get to know him right away," Cripe said. "He would occasionally call to ask me to lunch or breakfast to talk about volleyball and athletics. One day he said he was going to have a meeting in the office of administrators, and was going to talk about doing season tickets for volleyball. Reserved seating. He asked if I would like to come to the meeting. It was me and the head of marketing and ticketing and all of those people, event staff, with me being the only outsider. Someone asked me why I was there, and I said to talk about reserved seating for volleyball. One of the guys said, 'We'll never sell reserved seats for any women's sport at Nebraska.'

"In walks Bill Byrne, and he says, 'What are we not gonna do? We're not only going to do it, we're going to do it next weekend.'" And so it went. Fans could buy season tickets with reserved seats and the days of getting in free with a football ticket were over.

If you couldn't make it to a big match in person, other

viewing options were available, thanks to public television. It has been a major component in the volleyball program's popularity for forty-plus years. More specifically, Nebraska ETV (or NET), now known as Nebraska Public Media (NPM). Nebraska ETV started televising volleyball matches to a statewide audience in 1980.

Bill Doleman, a Fairbury, Nebraska, native who did many of the volleyball telecasts and has worked on broadcasts for everyone from NET to NBC, shared his thoughts on the history and significance of the partnership:

> Back at that time, Nebraska ETV was always looking for that angle to celebrate Nebraska, and it had one of the most sophisticated television operations in the country at the time. I think Nebraska ETV was at the forefront of television technology in figuring out ways to get the signal throughout the state, and when you have that capability and then you have the people who had the foresight to think how can we connect what we do to the people from Lincoln to Scottsbluff and all parts of the state. You look at the roster, and you see Ogallala and Sidney and it just made a lot of sense.
>
> I was blessed to have been able to call matches for NETV for about ten years, so I kind of had a front-row seat, although we usually sat on scaffolding behind the temporary bleachers. NETV was putting volleyball on at a time when the only other place to see the sport on TV with any regularity was on cable networks in California. There may have been a couple of other places like in Texas, but it was rare. I'm pretty confident in saying that because volleyball was the first real foothold for my career. I was a young kid in the business, but I was getting offers to work because there were so few who could call the sport well. I bet you could count on one hand and not use all fingers.

Chris Marlowe, who calls the Denver Nuggets, was the one who did the matches out west as well as the big national matches. And then there was us at little ol' Nebraska ETV.

Steve Alvis and Jim Carmichael, who have unfortunately passed away, were the ones who really pushed NETV to put it on the air as much as it did, which was only a few times a year. Still, it was far more than anyone else was doing. It was the best thing on NETV and they produced the sport better than other networks who attempted to put it on, including California. Of course, the fans in the Coliseum made for an incredible visual backdrop and atmosphere. They were as much the story as what was taking place on the court. If anyone was channel surfing back then and they stumbled onto the scene, I'm convinced they had to stop to see what it was all about. It was easy to appreciate the synergy of the athleticism of the women on the court and the passion of the fans in the Coliseum. I really believe NETV's commitment and approach to the sport had a significant impact in advancing the program and exploding the fan base. Just like the old saying, that little boys grew up wanting to play Husker football, NETV allowed girls within the state and region to grow up wanting to play Husker volleyball.

Nebraska Public Media producer Brock Lohr has seen the coverage take off over the years. "The attendance grew, but not everyone could make it to Lincoln to see the Huskers play, so NET's statewide broadcasts exposed the program to viewers across Nebraska."

Terry Pettit, on his "Inside the Coaching Mind" podcast, once said: "When people ask me why volleyball is so big in the state of Nebraska, I usually give them two reasons. The first is the job that NET has done presenting volleyball on television for four decades, and the second is John Baylor."

JB. That is how John Baylor is known to Husker fans, and his is quite a story. It's the journey of an international relations major from Stanford who once wanted to be an actor but ended up giving the performance of his life in 1994 calling college volleyball in his home state. He became the voice of the program, but Pettit wasn't sure what to make of Baylor in the beginning.

Starting in 1991, the matches had been carried by KFOR in Lincoln, with Harvey Watson on the call. Pettit said about the move to Lincoln's KLIN: "[Watson] actually did a good job," Pettit said, "so I was actually quite disappointed when we moved, and it wasn't our decision. It had something to do with the Athletic Department."

Under Byrne the broadcasts moved to the Husker Sports Network shortly after the arrival of JB in 1994. "The first time I met John was on the road, on our way to Purdue," Pettit said. "You get to know people on a road trip. I think we probably flew to Indianapolis and drove up to West Lafayette. I got to know him, and he was eager to learn. So it didn't take long for me to really enjoy John, and it was certainly a challenge initially for him."

Baylor would not disagree on the challenge part. "Terry wasn't particularly forthcoming," Baylor said. "He was still quite guarded and was also grudgingly tolerant of my arrival as the new play-by-play guy because they did have a really good play-by-play guy before then. Pettit didn't want to change, and understandably so. Bill Byrne is the one who made the call because he wanted all the sports under one roof." Baylor started the gig with an apprehensive head coach so he needed an ally. That ally was Cathy Noth.

You think Noth was just a great player and coach on the court? Baylor, who had done some baseball and basketball play-by-play at Stanford, will tell you without hesitation she had a lot to offer for a newbie volleyball broadcaster as well.

"She was very kind," he said. "We spent some time in the vans talking about things. There was no YouTube back then. I read some stuff. I talked to Cathy."

Noth, who was an assistant for the Huskers from 1988 to 1998, said: "JB had his style. That's what he knew. I taught him some volleyball terms. I taught him when there's a touch it's not called a deflection. Stuff like that, that he could learn about so he could announce the game with volleyball terms."

Baylor said the challenges went beyond simply a knowledge of the sport. "I was solo with no color commentator," he said, "and the equipment was really bulky, so my memory is that the equipment required at least two pieces of luggage, and then it was a phone line that was extremely unreliable. Many of the away arenas we're not equipped for our broadcast, nor did they even expect us to do a volleyball broadcast. I had to alert them ahead of time that we needed a phone line, and so it was a circus in many locations. For example, at Iowa State in 1994 they decided to play the match in the practice gym, which seated maybe 100. I mean, it was packed, and there was no phone line. The phone was in the locker room down the hall at least 250 feet away. So I had to find the phone line and bring the cord that extended 300 feet, then I had to use masking tape or duct tape and put it on top of the cord, because people are going to be walking down the hallway to get into the match. And they set me up with a card table.

"Another time when I was at Kansas they decided the day before we showed up to disconnect all the phone lines in the building because they assumed there would be no broadcast for a volleyball match, so they were doing some repairs, and there was no phone line. So for the first 45 minutes I'm yelling into a primitive cell phone, and I'm losing my voice. We somehow get reconnected with some sort of mobile cellular unit an hour into the match, but yeah, there were technical challenges."

Baylor developed quite a following, in part because of his offbeat sayings to describe certain moments and his emphatic "Kaboom!" call on big-time kills. Former Husker star Kim Behrends, from tiny Chappell, in western Nebraska, says, "Baylor has a special little spot in my heart. For some reason we connected, and I think it started on trips when we'd travel my freshman year [1997]. My parents would listen to a lot of our games on the radio and loved all of Baylor's sayings, so they started keeping track of some of their favorites."

At a team banquet, Behrends shared some of those favorites with the audience. Such as: "If *you're* a cardiologist, it's time to pass out the business cards." "Nebraska is blocking better than cholesterol." "This one is going to be over faster than a hiccup."

From 2000 to 2017 Baylor's broadcast partner was Diane Mendenhall, the Ogallala native and former Kansas Jayhawk who became the NU volleyball program's first director of operations in 2000. "We were together for eighteen seasons," Baylor said. "Diane is extremely gifted, not just knowledgeable, but funny and fun. She really helped develop the style of the broadcast with fun and humor and levity."

Mendenhall loved it. "It was interesting," she said, "because I was told I was like the third director of operations for volleyball in the country, so it was a new role. Under the new rule they wanted to make sure that you were not a coach. You could approach the huddle. You could sit on the bench. But you could not look like you were coaching. So really, once the match began, there was nothing for me to do. So JB was like 'Why don't you just get on the radio with me?' Typical JB. So I just put on the headset, and I said what do you want me to do, and he said just talk about what you see, so that's what I did. I'll never forget that next week, when I was back in Lincoln. A friend said she heard me on the radio. She said, 'You need to speak up. I like what you said.' I had no formal training. It was fun for me because when I became director of operations I kind of left that coaching role. It allowed me to kind of be a coach again. And JB, I felt like we were a great team and we had fun."

A lot of fun. And Pettit became quite a fan, too, even comparing Baylor to baseball broadcast legend Vin Scully in volleyball circles. "He's very good," Pettit said. "So earnest. I don't know of any volleyball coach that I ever competed against who wasn't very positive about John. He is not only loved by Nebraska fans, but I think opposing coaches who wanted their matches to be on radio. He's very forthright in what he sees. He's not cynical. He's not sarcastic. He calls it like it is."

His most recent partner, Lauren Cook (West), has been grateful for Baylor's experience and teaching. It's what he does full-time in helping high school students with their ACT and SAT prep work through his On To College business. "JB is a really good mentor," said Cook, a former Husker All-American at setter and daughter of Coach John Cook. And, by the way, she only refers to Cook as "Coach Cook," not "Dad."

"He gives me tips. When they first put me into the radio gig, they just threw me in and said 'Figure it out.' JB has really helped me become a better color commentator. He's just fun. He makes it fun. Half the time, I don't know what he's talking about or who he's talking about or what that joke even means. I've just learned to kind of laugh and accept it. That's just who JB is."

Baylor said of Lauren: "She likes my humor. I always like that when I have an audience. She's very candid, especially with her dad. She obviously knows the program inside and out and the sport."

Like Cathy Noth, who mentored Baylor back in 1994. He was a quick study and is now a huge hit with the fans on twenty-plus radio stations across Nebraska. "There will be Final Fours, and we will go on early during drive time, and you can just feel the whole state listening. It's pretty exciting." And a lot of fun, too. "The broadcasts are known for fun and levity and entertainment value, which makes me very proud," he said. "It's not just intense scientific clarification of what's occurring. We go off on various tangents that we find kind of amusing, and the audience for the most part bears with us."

Lindsay Wischmeier (Peterson), a former Husker captain who followed Mendenhall as the program's director of operations, has been on the call with Baylor many times over the years, often for road matches. "JB is one of a kind," she said. "He is our personal tour guide for every city/town/campus we visit. His knowledge of trivial facts is second to none. Baylor is a big part of why Nebraska Volleyball is so popular. What he provides the listeners with, from his intensity, excitement, and one-liners, is unmatched in our sport." At the end of every broadcast, Baylor signs off by saying: "My role tonight? Describe what I saw. Mission accomplished." He's been the beloved voice of the program since 1994, when his partners were bulky suitcases of equipment, 300-foot cords, and duct tape.

The Huskers had their voice and entered the 1995 season with Baylor, lots of momentum and support, and plenty of talent on the court. And also one mountain of a mission: getting to the top.

# First at Last

# 13

Let's start the story of the Huskers' 1995 season with a few fun facts about Christy Johnson. She wasn't sure volleyball was her thing. She wasn't sure Nebraska was her thing. She wasn't sure setting was her thing. But the thing is, Johnson, as a self-proclaimed nervous wreck, led Terry Pettit and the Huskers to their first National Championship.

When it happened on December 16, 1995, and Nebraska was at the top of the college volleyball world for the first time, Johnson was happy, yes. No doubt about it. But she will tell you to this day that relief won over happiness on that day in Amherst, Massachusetts. The pressure and stress of it all had become quite difficult to bear.

Christy Johnson (Lynch) had the weight of the state and twenty-plus years of program history on her shoulders. The team had not made it to the Final Four since 1990, and expectations were high in 1995. There was some heat on the senior setter from Omaha—Millard North High School, to be precise—and she felt it. But in her corner was one of the all-time Husker greats at middle blocker, a future Hall of Fame coach, and a team full of people who believed in her.

This team: seniors Johnson, Allison Weston, and Billie Winsett; juniors Kate Crnich, Maria Hedbeck, and Jen McFadden; sophomores Kim Legg and Lisa Reitsma; and freshmen Lisa

Avery, Denise Koziol, Jaime Krondak, Stacie Maser, Fiona Nepo, and Renee Saunders.

In high school their leader had started out as a softball player who was playing volleyball on the side. She said Millard North's volleyball coach, Deb Grafentin, was a big influencer as Christy started thinking about changing her focus. "Just a tremendous coach," she said. Her club coach, Disa Johnson, a former All-American at Illinois, also had a big influence. "Had those two coaches not come into my life I don't think I would've even gotten into volleyball."

While there are many Husker volleyball stars who grew up with it, wanting to be part of it, Johnson wasn't one of them. "My experience was really different because I wasn't really into Nebraska Volleyball," she said. "They didn't recruit me very hard, didn't really need a setter when I was going through the process. I don't think I even went to a game before my senior year. It wasn't really my world at that time."

It was actually around the time Nebraska was playing in the Final Four in 1990 when Johnson decided to commit. "It all happened pretty late and kind of last minute," she said. "I'm pretty thankful. It worked out really well." But not without plenty of patience. Johnson had to wait her turn to be the Husker setter, behind Nikki Stricker (Best), who had a great story of her own. Stricker, a former middle blocker from Lincoln East, had an outstanding run as a Husker. She was a three-time all-conference honoree and the Big Eight Player of the Year as a senior in 1993.

In 1994, with Stricker gone, Johnson got her big chance, and she made the most of it. "It was just kind of a long time coming. I had been dreaming of being a setter for three years by then, so it was a really long process to become a starter. It was a really hard process mentally, really difficult to hang in there that long. So when I finally got that opportunity it was so much fun."

The Huskers won their first 31 matches in 1994, only losing 6 games in the process, and got to the Regional Finals before falling to Penn State in four sets in Lincoln. That team had three All-Americans: Johnson, Weston, and Kelly Aspegren. The disappointment was tempered with high hopes for 1995, when Johnson and Weston would be seniors. Weston was also from the Omaha area, the first of many Husker standouts from Papillion, Nebraska.

Before the season, Pettit shared this forecast with anyone who would listen, and more people were starting to listen: "We certainly should be strong," Pettit said. "We have great senior leadership in Allison Weston, Billie Winsett, and Christy Johnson. We were 31-1 last season, and I think we're going to be better this year."

Tougher, too. Like the cover of the 1995 media guide showing the three seniors wearing sweat and don't-mess-with-us expressions. Two Nebraskans and Winsett, who, like her coach, hailed from Indiana. And a few words to play by: *One Goal. One Focus. One Champion.*

Winsett was an outside hitter from Boonville, Indiana. The Huskers also had a dynamic outside in Reitsma, who was a sophomore from Sanborn, Iowa, along with a freshman setter who was Johnson's understudy and a big-time fan favorite from Honolulu, Fiona Nepo. And it certainly didn't hurt having Cathy Noth on the bench alongside Pettit.

In his book *Talent and the Secret Lives of Teams*, Pettit writes:

> Five of our starters were typical Nebraska Volleyball student athletes. They were from the Midwest, (four within a six-hour drive from Lincoln), exceptional students, and technically very efficient with their volleyball skills. Four of them would receive All-American recognition. Billie Winsett became NCAA Woman of the Year, Allison Weston

was co-winner of the Honda Broderick Award as the outstanding college volleyball player of 1995, and the setter, Christy Johnson, led Nebraska to a 62-2 record in her junior and senior years while never losing an away match. Lisa Reitsma, a sophomore right-side player, earned All-American honors her final three seasons, and a fifth starter, Jen McFadden, the middle blocker who played opposite Weston, was one of the most intimidating blockers in college volleyball. We also had an exceptional defensive specialist, Maria Hedbeck, a junior from Sollentuna, Sweden. It was the sixth starter that I had concerns about. Her name was Kate Crnich.

Kate Crnich (Riggins), a junior outside from Illinois, was not the headliner on the roster, but oh, would that punk rocker from Chicagoland become a star when all was said and won. "I was not really heavily recruited," she said. "I would be considered very raw. I never went to a weight room until I was in college, or my summer before college. They sent me to a summer weight program and I had to join a gym. My technique was all backward, so there was a lot of work to do. I always had a great arm swing, so I think that's kind of how I got recruited."

Crnich said Pettit made it clear she wasn't going to come in and start right away. "The other schools, Rhode Island and Alabama, were saying, 'Oh, immediately you're going to be our star player.'" She said the other schools also talked about their towns and the social life while Nebraska was talking about academic support. "That's why I chose Nebraska."

It was a life-changer of a choice, as it turned out. Not only because of what happened in 1995, when she became a starter for the first time, but that was a big part of it. "We just had great leadership that year," Crnich said. "Christy, from the beginning, said 'This is our time, and I'm going to do everything I can to win.' Christy said she was going to take care of herself, and not so much of a social life, get good sleep. She just said she would appreciate it if others did the same. We kind of knew this was our time."

They weren't thinking, "Wouldn't it be great if we won?" They were thinking, "We got this." *One Goal. One Focus. One Champion.*

In 1995 the Huskers lost their second match of the season, 3–1, to Stanford at the Coliseum, but they never lost again. That didn't mean there weren't moments, even in victory, when the pressure weighed on Johnson. One of those moments came in Norman, Oklahoma, near the end of the regular season in mid-November. "We were at Oklahoma, and we win in three, and I find her crying on the stairs," Pettit said. "She says, 'Coach, I know I didn't set well tonight. I let my teammates down.' I said, 'Christy, you're the reason they play hard. You're the reason they play well.' That was something she had to work through and she did. We really developed her in terms of leadership. It's important to have a leader who is capable of holding everybody else accountable, and it took a while to get her to that point, but her senior year, she did."

Pettit said Johnson would throw a player out of a drill if they were not playing hard. Reitsma was one of the players Johnson had to be tough on at times. "The coaches really got on the seniors to hold everyone accountable and to push all of us to do our best," Reitsma said of Pettit, Noth, and Todd Raasch, a Wisner, Nebraska, native who also coached at Nebraska–Kearney. "We were basically getting on each other's nerves and kind of falling apart as a team, until we finally had a team meeting off the court that made us confront each other, and that brought us even closer and made us even stronger than before. The three seniors were so determined and so focused to win it all. It was amazing to watch."

Winsett provided a good portion of that determination. "Billie's greatest strength was her will," Pettit said. "She just stayed with everything until she got it right, so much so that if she missed a pass or a serve, she wouldn't rotate out. She would just stay there until she got it."

And then there was Weston, who played volleyball, basketball, and soccer at Papillion–La Vista High School. She also ran track. "I didn't hone in on volleyball until really my junior year of high school. So many kids are focusing on two and maybe just the one sport all year long. I played a lot of different sports and got coached by lots of different coaches and played with lots of different people and worked on developing skill sets and that kind of stuff through all the various seasons. I think they really helped me stay healthy, for one, and you don't burn out."

She also said a former Husker had a lot to do with her success in high school and beyond. "I think the biggest thing was that my high school coach was Gwen Egbert. She was a tremendous coach. She was instrumental in, for one, teaching the fundamentals and just being a huge advocate for challenging yourself and putting yourself in the best position to have success. By the time I was a junior, I decided that volleyball was the sport I wanted to pursue in college, although I was recruited a little bit for basketball. But by then it was, 'Yeah, volleyball's the track I'd like to go down.' And it worked out quite well."

Yes it did. Weston, a 6-foot middle blocker, was a three-time First-Team All-American—the first in program history—and a future Olympian and U.S. team captain. She was also an Academic All-American. One of the top Huskers of all time. Her 1,778 career kills, including 487 in 1995, was still no. 2 in Husker history through the 2022 season. And she also still held the Nebraska record for most kills in a four-set match, with 37 against Colorado in 1994. She was the co-

National Player of the year in 1995, along with Cary Wendell of Stanford. And in 2015 she was inducted into the University of Nebraska Athletic Hall of Fame.

Yes, it worked out quite well for Weston, who is quick to credit the players who came before her. One of them was Stephanie Thater, a middle who was also a three-time All-American (1990–92). "She was a senior my freshman year. A middle blocker, and I trained as a middle blocker, and she was so intimidating. She was so good, and she hit the ball so hard. I was like, 'Wow, I get to train with this every single day.' So she was very motivating. She was very encouraging. A good teammate to have and to learn from."

Weston said a primary key for the Huskers in 1995 was team camaraderie. "It was a grind. We worked hard. Pettit ran a tight ship. Every single day of practice we worked hard. You had your teammates to rely on. Everybody was focused on winning and continuing the tradition and having success both on the court and in the classroom. Academics were always a high priority. Everybody got along very well. We were very goal-oriented. Obviously, looking back to the '95 season, with as much focus as we had on winning a National Championship, I don't think I've ever been part of a team that's been so driven and so committed to a goal. That's probably the biggest thing that I remember. Every day in practice working and trying to replicate the intensity of a match, and that's really hard to do in practice every day."

Weston said Johnson and another Husker setter had a lot to do with that focus in practice. "Christy worked so hard with all of her setting skills and footwork. Just a highly motivated person, and all the setters who came before. Val [Novak]. Cathy Noth. Having played there and having been a very successful coach there. It was invaluable having a coach on the staff who had played there and understood the program and played for the head coach, too. That makes a pretty big difference with the dynamics."

Those setters, including Nepo, were there for Weston. There was just one thing they couldn't help her with. Cartwheels. One of the greatest athletes in Nebraska history couldn't do a cartwheel to save her life. "We always did cartwheels for warm-ups, and I couldn't do them until my senior year," she said. "I kind of finally got one."

A national title, too. Thanks to three key ingredients, according to Johnson. Senior leadership: "Billie, Allison and I talked about the goal of winning it all and were very focused on that goal all year." Preparation: "Nebraska had been knocking on the door for years, so in ways it was years of hard work of those who came before us that prepared us. We were experienced, and Coach Pettit had prepared us very well to play those high-level teams." Role acceptance. "Everyone on our team contributed in different ways, and everyone played their role so well." Starting with the seniors. Noth said the grit of Johnson, Weston, and Winsett set the championship tone. "They had their roles, and the team was very aware who was in charge of what," Noth said. "They pushed the younger players to a higher standard, and they caught on fast."

The Huskers opened the NCAA Tournament with a bye, followed by home victories over George Mason and Penn State. The four-gamer against the Nittany Lions provided some revenge after the 1994 loss and was capped with a 15–2 exclamation point in the fourth-set clincher. The Huskers then swept UCLA in the Regional Final at the Coliseum.

Nebraska was rolling like a snowball heading to the Final Four in Amherst, and that was part of the story. Snow, and lots of it. Even short trips by bus could be challenging, so Pettit elected to move the Huskers from Springfield—twenty-five miles away—to the UMass campus. "That was critical,"

Pettit said. "Otherwise, you are spending a couple of hours to go over a mountain to get to this university."

Weston said the move helped in more ways than one. "We were just kind of hunkered down," Weston said, "and I remember thinking, This is a strange way to prepare for a National Championship match. It's just kind of hanging out in a student motel on campus, waiting for the games to start, but that was just one more thing of 'Let's just make the best of it and go out and do this.'"

In the semifinals on Thursday, December 14, No. 4 Texas faced top-ranked Stanford, and No. 2 Nebraska met No. 3 Michigan State. Both matches went 5 sets. Texas superstar Demetria Sance, just a freshman at the time, had 25 kills in the Longhorns' victory over the Cardinal. Nebraska had its hands full with the Spartans, who had made the Final Four for the first time. The Huskers won 10–15, 15–8, 15–8, 9–15, 15–8. The score was tied 7–7 in the fifth before Nebraska zapped Michigan State with four consecutive points. Weston led the Huskers with 30 kills. Johnson simply led.

John Baylor, still fairly new to the Husker radio gig at the time, remembers it well. Blizzard and all. "That match was a marathon and could've gone either way. Christy Johnson exerted more energy between points than during points," Baylor said. "Those post-rally celebrations telegraphed her enthusiasm and belief to her teammates and to Michigan State, a message that bolstered her team and dispirited the Spartans."

Johnson was battling those Spartans and the what-ifs in that fifth set. "I was starting to get really nervous, really freaking out," she said. "What if I screw up? I was able to calm my mind and kind of get back to all the stuff I had been working on. And then we kind of made a couple of great rallies, a couple of great plays, saved a couple balls, and then went on to win that set. For me personally that was a huge turning point, because once we got through that, and once Texas beat

Stanford, I felt better because we had already beaten Texas, and we already lost to Stanford. I think I went into the Texas match just a little more confident."

Not only had they beaten Texas, but they swept Texas, in Austin, in early November. "There were a lot of advantages in Texas winning that match," Pettit said. "From a scouting standpoint, understanding their personnel and what they could do." Not the typical neckwear for snowstorms, Hawaiian leis were part of the attire for the coaches and several Husker supporters that weekend, thanks to the Nepo family. The Fiona Fan Club was bigger than ever. Nepo, though just a freshman, was already playing a key role, as a player and as a teammate, helping keep things loose. She only had 38 set assists that year playing behind Johnson, but Nepo led the team in comic relief.

"Quite the character," Weston said. "We obviously had our scouting report, and the coaches would come in, and we would go over the rotations, but Fiona, once the coaches left, would bring her own special flair to preparing. I wish I could remember the details, but I think there was some singing, maybe some chanting. I definitely credit her with keeping things light and fun and positive. For a freshman that's a huge role to take on. Everybody just appreciated it and laughed and kept the levity there."

Reitsma said the team was "amazed" by Fiona's talent and personality. "She was an amazing athlete, but she had such a relaxed, fun side to her, and somehow she had Coach Pettit wrapped around her little finger."

Reitsma, a 6-foot-4 right-side, was showing some amazing skills of her own. She was among the team leaders in kills, blocks, and serving. Only Hedbeck, with 29, had more aces than Reitsma's 25. Reitsma was one of only three Huskers to play in all 33 matches and all 106 games that year, joining Weston and Winsett in that category.

Winsett, known best for her defense—she led the team with 290 digs in 1995—had become more of an offensive force in her last season, with 319 kills and a .302 hitting percentage. "Prior to her senior year we changed a fundamental with her, which you normally wouldn't do," Pettit said. "She had a traditional arm swing, where there was total shoulder rotation, and so I went with a more European arm swing, primarily an elbow-wrist snap, which allowed her to hit higher so the ball didn't have as much force, but she could pretty much hit it wherever she wanted to."

Pettit said that technique was crucial in Amherst. Winsett had 19 kills and 16 digs against Michigan State and again rose to the occasion against Texas in the championship match. "Most players, you wouldn't ask to change something that critical going into their senior season. But if we hadn't changed that [with Winsett], that wouldn't have happened. Texas was in a hybrid defense, where they rotated with two players digging line, and Billie was able to hit shots and snap that wrist that would fall just short of the angle there." Noth described Winsett as a "quiet leader who didn't need a lot of attention. She led by positivity and steadiness in her play. Steady Eddie."

Winsett and Crnich, both 5-foot-11, were not designated as the go-to attackers before the title match. Not with the All-Americans Weston and Reitsma on the floor. But that is what happened, and it happened, according to their floor leader, because Billie and Kate knew their roles and knew that meant being ready for anything. "We had never had a game plan to feed our outside hitters a ton of balls," Johnson said. "We were a more middle and right-side offensive team. It was evident that Texas was keying on our middles and especially Weston. We responded by going more to Kate and Billie, and they both were ready and prepared for that moment. Once they both started getting a lot of kills, we figured to just keep going to them. It didn't seem like a big deal.

We didn't feel panic or that we were in trouble. It was more like, 'This is going to be Billie and Kate's night,' and they were confident and ready. We all had total confidence they could carry the offensive load that night."

That night the announced attendance in Amherst, despite the bad weather, was 7,364, with plenty of red in the house. The total attendance for the 1995 tournament was a record 100,565. The match was televised by ESPN2 (and highlights are still available on YouTube).

The Huskers fell behind quickly in the first set, with Texas taking a 12–4 lead out of the gate. But Nebraska showed a lot of fight at the end of game one before falling, 15–11. That provided the momentum that helped the Huskers cruise to a 15–2 win in game two. They were strong in the third as well, winning 15–7.

With the Longhorns set up to stop Weston and Reitsma, Crnich and Winsett came through with kill after kill. They finished with 25 apiece. Crnich, who had a total of 185 kills for the season with a .237 hitting percentage, hit .500 that night. The 25 kills were a career high. That sixth starter that Pettit had concerns about in the preseason had a good night. The best.

Steve Sipple, a longtime Nebraska sports journalist, was representing the *Lincoln Journal Star* that night. "[Crnich] did what she had to do in a big way. That was the story, I thought. It wasn't the only story, but Kate Crnich had a gigantic match."

Johnson said Kate was just a great teammate who rose to the occasion when it mattered most. "I know that Coach Pettit talked to Kate before the Final Four and expressed his trust and belief in her, and I think that allowed her to relax and just play. Kate didn't seem to second-guess herself, she would just go after it and play hard."

Crnich, with a story that a coach in any sport should share, demonstrated the importance of putting in the work even if you are not the star, because you never know when you might need to be the star. "I never thought really this was going to be the match of my life. Just with all the training that you do. There are nerves there, of course. We got all of our nerves out, and it was just something we knew we were going to do.

"Christy and I just clicked, and Billie as well. We all clicked together. We just made it work. It just kind of happened. I just thought, I don't want to let anyone down. I don't want to let my teammates down."

With the Huskers up 2 sets to 1, the fourth game was a back-and-forth battle that finally ended 16–14 when Sance was blocked by Weston and Johnson, a couple of Nebraska girls who did what they came to do—win a national title, the program's first. Now, if anyone was still doubting the power of Nebraska Volleyball, this group gave notice as the first team from the Midwest to win it all *One Goal. One Focus. One Champion.*

In the championship, Nebraska won 11–15, 15–2, 15–7, 16–14 and outhit Texas .296 to .183. Weston, who had 18 kills while hitting a rough .040, didn't have to have a big night on the attack. Instead, she came through with 9 block assists and a career-high 22 digs. Reitsma had 16 kills and hit .484. McFadden also provided big support, with 16 kills (.414).

Coach Pettit led both teams in flying clipboards and was just glad he didn't kill anyone with that saucer he sent to the skies in celebration as soon as the last point was made. His team was a National Champion, and after some of the hoopla died down that night, he needed to make a phone call. It was before most folks had cell phones, so Pettit had to find a pay phone. He wanted to call his dad back home in Indiana. "He answered the phone and he said, 'How'd your day go?' That's my dad's sense of humor."

Weston said the 1995 season "was a grind, but it all was worth it in the end. We set the highest goal you could possibly imagine and achieved it." Cartwheels and all. With a mountain of credit going to her setter. "Christy was definitely the glue that held the team together and kept everyone focused," Weston said. "She put forth so much energy to keep everybody focused and execute and perform."

Media followers noticed, too. "That season Terry Pettit had asked her to be a tough leader rather than a nurturing friend," John Baylor said, "and she had honored his request all the way until the final point. She was one of the greatest winners and Huskers ever, especially in 1995." She had 87 assists that night against Texas, and that's still a record at Nebraska for a four-set match—regular season or postseason. Her 13.90 assists per game that year is only topped by her 14.17 in 1994. "Christy Johnson knew what to do," Sipple said. "She always knew what to do. I was always struck by how emotional she was. I know she would not accept losing."

Every other team in the country had to accept a loss at the end in 1995. Not the Huskers, and not their leader, who went 63-2 without losing a road match as the team's starting setter. No. 63 was the best one. For Johnson it was time to take that big red balloon of emotions and set it free, as a champion.

Crnich, with nothing but admiration and gratitude, was just glad she could help. "Gosh, I owe everything to her. She's the reason why I did what I did, tried to be responsible and worked my butt off in practice and not miss anything, and try to get along with everybody. She was so good at communication on and off the court. I remember feeling, 'I don't want to let her down, she works her butt off, she's making all the calls, and she's counting on us.' I don't remember feeling a lot of stress and pressure. I know she did." But it was time to exhale. Finally.

"I hate saying it," Johnson said, "but my first feeling was relief. You want to just say utter joy, but I was such an anxious player, I was just obsessed with it. It was such a high-pressure high-anxiety time for me. But when it finally happened I felt like I could relax. I could finally not worry about this. In a perfect world I would've wished for a much different emotion, but that's just how I felt—'Thank goodness we did that.' And then, after that, just joy and happiness, just really happy for my coaches and teammates and the fans."

After celebrating in Amherst, the champions got a big welcome from the home crowd at the Coliseum the next day. "The fans were pretty amazing, the ones who were able to make it there [to the Final Four], and then coming back home to Lincoln, having a celebration at the Coliseum. It was really cool to see that many people so excited.

"That's a pretty cool thing that sports can do." That's a pretty cool thing, what Johnson did, leading Nebraska Volleyball to its first National Championship. "That's something I'll always remember," she said, "being at the Coliseum during that celebration in the crowd, just seeing how happy everybody was." On top of the world.

# 14

# Thanksgiving

When Nebraska won the National Championship in volleyball for the first time, Nancy Grant Colson soaked it all in while watching from home in Lincoln. One of Terry Pettit's first Huskers, she wasn't there, but actually, she was. "I remember the cameras showing Terry throwing his clipboard up in the air after the block on the incredible Demetria Sance, for the win. I remember thinking how happy Cathy Noth looked—for the team, and for Terry. I recall not being surprised at the outcome of the match. I had had the opportunity to work Husker camps with Christy, Allison, and Billie, and they were just so humble, paid attention to detail, and just plain showed up, no matter what the task, at camp each day. Terry spoke so highly of them. I guess, finally, I know I felt a sense of pride that two of the incredible players and leaders in the march to the National Championship were Nebraska kids: Christy Johnson and Allison Weston."

Texas head coach Mick Haley paid the Huskers a meaningful compliment after the match when he said: "This is a great experience for our team, but I wonder if our players know how hard it is for seniors to lead a team while still playing well. Nebraska understands that." And Weston understood that Pettit's wisdom was at the center of it all. "A very, very smart person," she said. "He could really read players and get them to do the best they could. Sometimes you'd have meetings with him, and it would be spooky how he was in your mind. He knows exactly what you're thinking and how to have a discussion and get the best out of you.

"In the gym, precision detail with lots of skill training. I just remember in two-a-days, we would break up into positions and work on skills over and over. He was such a good teacher. For someone who hadn't really played the game much, it's kind of remarkable that he could coach it so well, especially with setters. Just a very skillful, knowledgeable person."

He got the most from that 1995 team, and Husker Hall of Famer Karen Dahlgren (Schonewise) was there in Amherst on the night it all came together, as the head coach at Kansas. "The annual coaches convention is run in conjunction with the tournament, so I happened to be there for that historic championship. It was just pure joy to see them win that match!"

Pure joy was also the mood back in Lincoln at the Coliseum the next day. Kari Beckenhauer said it was quite a celebration for the returning champions. "You need to remember that the internet was just in its infancy in 1995, and likewise for cell phones," she said. "There were many fans who attended the game in Amherst, but fans were mobilized locally after it was announced that the team would meet the public on Sunday afternoon at the Coliseum, free for anyone to attend. The Match Club also had a phone number that contained a voice message about this gathering, so people could call it to get the latest info.

"The Huskers had played a regional at the Coliseum prior to the Final Four, so the west and east sides of the balconies had huge NCAA banners that said 'NCAA National Championships.' Someone from athletics had crossed out the last few letters, so the sign read 'NCAA National Champions.' The place was packed to the rafters. People were hanging by their toes to see the National Champs. Some small risers were placed on the floor facing the south. The mayor of Lincoln [Mike Johanns] was there, along with the governor [Ben Nelson]. The crowd, being impatient, started chanting, 'Coach, coach, open the door—let those Huskers on the floor.' First the coaches entered. Next, many of the reserve players entered and stood on the risers, then the regular subs and then the starters—with Allison Weston carrying the trophy. The crowd roared, clapped, screamed, took pictures, jumped up and down, hugged and high-fived each other, mainly because the Huskers had been so close to winning the National Title a few times before. All of the dignitaries spoke, Pettit spoke, and the three captains spoke.

"People hung around, took pictures of players with their kids, pictures of players with themselves. No selfies. Everyone had to use a real camera with film! People had T-shirts autographed, arms autographed, hugs were exchanged, phone numbers were exchanged, etcetera. Total mayhem for some time!"

Post-mayhem, in the quiet of the days that followed, Kathi DeBoer (Wieskamp)

called Pettit to let him know what it meant to her. "I said it felt like it was me, and I was part of it. I said it felt like I won. He said, 'You did, and every other player who was part of the steps to get here had a piece of that championship.'"

Jan Zink was one of those players, one of the very first, and to see the program reach the top was the ultimate in ceiling crashing. A breakthrough for the program and for volleyball in Nebraska and the Midwest. "It just showed that volleyball had come so far in Nebraska," Zink said. "With the high school coaches, even the club teams at that time, they were pretty young, but all of that was really increasing the level of play here in Nebraska. And a lot of those girls were from Nebraska, so that made it even more exciting. I was proud. Very proud."

Crowd estimates for the championship celebration at the Coliseum ranged from 3,000 to 3,500. Zink and her teammates played in front of much smaller crowds, but what a thrill it was to see 8,000 or on their feet to honor the 1974 and 1975 Husker teams during a match at the Devaney Center in late October 2022. It was a night to honor and thank many of the players and coaches who had started it all. And it was a big night for the author, too. I got to meet Pat Sullivan in person for the first time that night. A thrill, for sure.

It was coming up on Thanksgiving, which is always the time when the Nebraska Volleyball season really gets good, with the end of the regular season and NCAA tournament selections coming soon and all of the high hopes that come with that second season and the holidays, too. Gratitude abounds. A lot of thanks to give as we wrap up volume one and twenty-five years of Husker history—to Zink and Colson and Dahlgren and so many others who have shared their stories for this project. It is their story, after all.

Big thanks to Sullivan, Pettit, and John Cook, for all they have done (and are still doing). There is no Nebraska Volleyball story without those three. Same for one legend I didn't get to talk to—the late Dr. Barbara Hibner, a hero to so many at Nebraska.

Lindsay Wischmeier (Peterson), the pride of Lewiston, Nebraska, is high on the gratitude list. She is a former Husker standout who will never get enough credit for all she has done for the program—as a player and as the team's director of operations since 2006. I probably contacted her fifty times asking for help, and she got back to me every time. There might just be a Lewiston chapter in volume two. Thanks, Wisch.

Thanks to my wife, Anna, who loves her Husker Volleyball and wouldn't let me give up on this project, even when the pandemic and work and other life challenges got in the way. Her love and support is through the roof, roof, roof.

Thanks to Rob Taylor at the University of Nebraska Press, for plenty of patience during this journey, which is not over. I will try to hit a deadline volume two, Rob, I promise. Grateful for the assistance of Nate Pohlen, Bonnie Ryan Matt Smith, Scott Bruhn, and everyone with Nebraska Athletics Communications, all of whom helped me with facts and interviews and photos.

From here to Tokyo, I am grateful for the support of Jordan Larson, who had just turned nine years old when the Huskers won that first title. Even while winning an Olympic gold medal she made plenty of time for this project. Not once did she say she was too busy to help. More to come on the GOAT. You can count on it.

It all started with Kathy Drewes and Vicki Highstreet sharing memories with me in the kitchen at the home of Kari and Tom Beckenhauer. All four of them have been invaluable resources here. And thanks to my coworkers at the Food Bank of Lincoln for their support, always. I get to talk volleyball often with former Huskers Colson and Deb (Mueller) Headley. Both are regular volunteers at the Food Bank.

We also had a Husker supporter in Gaylord, Michigan. In my role as a fundraiser, I noticed in the summer of 2022 that the Food Bank had received a very generous estate gift from Gaylord, in the northern part of the Wolverine State. The donor was the late Margaret Penney. The name sounded familiar. Wouldn't it be something if it was *that* Margaret Penney, the woman who coached the volleyball Huskers for two years before Pat Sullivan, just as Title IX was starting to take hold?

I found the obituary through the Nelson Funeral Home, and this is how it read:

Margaret Anne Penney, 89, of Gaylord, Michigan passed away Tuesday, December 7, 2021. She was born the daughter of Cyril and Mable (Bough) Penney in Royal Oak, MI, June 21, 1932. Margaret received her bachelor's and master's degree from the University of Michigan. She moved to Lincoln, Nebraska in 1962, where she worked as an associate professor in physical education at the University of Nebraska. Margaret was instrumental in creating intermural women's volleyball, eventually growing it into intercollegiate in Nebraska.

And look at how it has grown since. I have to believe Margaret was pretty proud of what happened in 1995. Record crowds—the 11,529 fans who watched the Huskers sweep Colorado at the Devaney Center to set an NCAA record at the time—and the program's first National Championship and all the triumphant stories that came with it.

The story of Kate Crnich (Riggins) is certainly one of my favorites. A punk-rock fan (Ramones, Buzzcocks, Social Distortion, to name a few), she became a rock star at Nebraska. She also met her husband in Lincoln, and there is a story there too.

It was April of 1996. Jack Riggins was out with a buddy. Kate was out with friend and teammate Maria Hedbeck. One thing led to another, and Jack asked Kate out for a movie night. Jack's friends in Naval ROTC found out and said that was very cool he had a date with Kate Crnich. He wasn't sure about what a big deal it was until those same friends showed him a poster of the 1995 National Champions. "So when I picked her up that night, one of the first things I said was 'I have to apologize. I remember you saying you played volleyball. I thought you meant like, intramurals.'"

A little more than intramurals, yep. The Huskers were the defending National Champs, in large part because of his date and future wife. The program made a Nebraskan out of Kate Crnich. She and Jack, a Navy SEAL who has helped Husker teams as a "cultural dynamics advisor" and their four kiddos call Lincoln home. "You really do feel all of the love the fans have for this game and the team," she said, before repeating a comment she shared with Pettit during her playing days. "When I stepped on the Coliseum court for the first time, I sensed that something special was happening to me and that I would never be the same again."

And Thanksgivings in Nebraska will never be the same again. Just ask a pilgrim from the village of Plymouth. "It seems like only a blink ago that we were there, playing at Nationals," said Drewes. "Sometimes I smile as I think to myself, 'We sure started something back then.'"

Something special. With more to come. Much more.